# Acting on Principle

**An examination of race and
ethnicity in social services provision
for children and families**

Ravinder Barn
Ruth Sinclair
Dionne Ferdinand

**B** *r i t i s h*
**A** *g e n c i e s*
*f o r* **A** *d o p t i o n*
*a n d* **F** *o s t e r i n g*

UNITING BRITAIN
COMMISSION FOR
RACIAL EQUALITY
FOR A JUST SOCIETY

Published by
**British Agencies for Adoption & Fostering**
(BAAF)
Skyline House
200 Union Street
London SE1 0LX

Charity registration 275689

Commissioned for the
**Commission for Racial Equality**

© CRE 1997

British Library Cataloguing in Publication Data
A catalogue record for this book is available
from the British Library

ISBN 1 873868 40 5

Designed by Andrew Haig & Associates
Typeset by Avon Dataset Ltd, Bidford on
Avon, Warwickshire B50 4JH
Printed by Russell Press (TU), Nottingham

# The Authors

### Dr Ravinder Barn

Dr Ravinder Barn is Lecturer in Applied Social Studies at Royal Holloway, University of London. She has published widely in the areas of race, ethnicity and child care. Her book, *Black Children in the Public Care System*, was published by Batsford/BAAF in 1993.

### Dr Ruth Sinclair

Dr Ruth Sinclair is Director of Research at the National Children's Bureau. She is author of several publications in child care. Her recent co-authored contributions include *Social Work and Assessment with Adolescents*, NCB, and *Planning to Care: Regulation, Procedure and Practice under the Children Act 1989*, NCB.

### Dionne Ferdinand

Dionne Ferdinand was Research Assistant to this study. Prior to this post, she worked as Research Officer in the Race Equality Unit, London Borough of Hackney while studying for an MA in Social Policy and Administration at Goldsmiths College, University of London. Dionne was diagnosed with cancer in 1993, and died at the age of 29, in 1996. This report is a tribute to her young life.

# The Advisory Group

| | |
|---|---|
| **Khurshid Ahmed** | Assistant Chief Executive Head of Equal Opportunities Unit Birmingham City Council |
| **Gwen Caesar** | Freelance Researcher |
| **Bharti Dhir** | Senior Social Worker Formerly with Newham Borough Council, now works for Hammersmith and Fulham |
| **David Divine** | Freelance Consultant, formerly Assistant Director, CCETSW |
| **Toyin Okitikpi** | Lecturer in Social Work, West London Institute, Brunel University |

# Acknowledgements

This report is the outcome of a research project funded by the Commission for Racial Equality (CRE). We wish to acknowledge the support of the CRE and the Advisory Group appointed to offer their expertise.

Our thanks are also due to the local authority social services departments which took part in this study. We are grateful to social work practitioners and managers for their help and support in providing useful information regarding agency policies and procedures, and for giving us time to be interviewed in spite of their pressurised work schedules.

We would like to express our special thanks to parents, carers and young people who spoke to us so very openly and honestly of their experiences of social service provision.

A number of other individuals deserve a mention: Dr Paul Pal for his help and assistance with quantitative data analysis; Ratna Dutt, Shaila Shah, Marcia Spencer, Joe Charlesworth, Phil Barnett, Judith Hanna, Jean Cousins, Julie Bailey and David Berridge for their helpful comments on earlier drafts. Also, particular thanks go to Shaila Shah, Head of Communications at BAAF, for her useful editorial input. A special debt of gratitude is owed to Colin Hann, Head of Corporate and Strategy Unit, CRE, for his support and "staying power" throughout this study, and to Greville Percival, CRE, for ensuring the smooth running of the financial wheels.

In memory of **Dionne Ferdinand** (1966–1996), co-author and research assistant to this project, who died of cancer. She will be greatly missed.

# Glossary

**Asian** – The term Asian is used to refer to those of South Asian background, who themselves or whose ancestors originate from the Indian Sub-continent. The terms Chinese and Vietnamese are used separately so as to not create confusion under the general category of Asian.

**Black** – the term black is used in its political context to refer to those who share a common, but not necessarily similar, experience on the basis of their "race", colour and ethnic origin in Britain. In this study, it refers to individuals of African-Caribbean, Asian, African, mixed parentage, and Chinese/Vietnamese origin. Ethnic distinctions are made wherever necessary and relevant. Also, the term "minority ethnic" is used interchangeably with black.

**Looked after** – The term looked after refers to children in local authority care who are accommodated with parental or child consent and those in care following court proceedings. The terms "in care", and "in the public care system" are also used in this report to refer to children looked after by local authorities.

**Mixed parentage** – Mixed parentage is used to refer to individuals of mixed racial and cultural origins. In the study, the majority of such children had a white indigenous mother and an African-Caribbean/African father.

**Race** – The word "race" is placed in inverted commas in the text to stress that the categorisation of people into different "races" is a social definition – one which has been used to determine hierarchies which have disadvantaged black people. It is not a biological definition as there is only one race, the human race. It is used here in the absence of a suitable alternative.

**White** – The term white is used to refer to both white indigenous and white European. The majority of white children in this study were white indigenous, including those of white Irish background.

# Contents

# Figures and Tables

## Figures

## Tables

# Foreword

## Sir Herman Ouseley, Chairman, Commission for Racial Equality

The Children Act 1989 was a landmark in defining the way social services departments meet the needs of ethnic minority people. It placed a new duty on local authorities to 'give due consideration' to children's 'religious persuasion, racial origin and cultural and linguistic background' in making decisions about them. Local authorities needed to measure this new responsibility alongside their existing duty under the Race Relations Act to avoid racial discrimination and to promote equality of opportunity. The new legal provision and the supporting guidance from the Department of Health marked an official end to those 'colour blind' policies and practices which, by ignoring relevant differences, could reflect and reinforce any underlying racism of social institutions. For, if children constitute a vulnerable group in our society, children whose needs are badly misinterpreted or who are at risk of exclusion and rejection because of their colour or ethnic origin are particularly vulnerable.

Over the years, there have been persistent, serious worries about the way the child care system has responded – or failed to respond – to the needs and interests of the different ethnic groups which make up British society. Top of the list are:

- that proportionately, the numbers of ethnic minority children in care are significantly higher than the number of such children in the general population;

- that such children are in institutional *residential* care for too long, perhaps because of the priority given to placing children with families of the same ethnic group;

- that social services have been failing effectively to meet the cultural and religious needs of ethnic minority children (and families);

- that social services have not responded well because there are far too few social workers of ethnic minority backgrounds.

Given these concerns, the findings presented in the study are, perhaps inevitably, mixed.

The three case study local authorities had been successful in recruiting foster carers from a wide range of ethnic groups. The result was that, for a clear majority of children in the research sample, it had been possible to find a placement with a family of the same background. Only 15 per cent of children in the sample were in residential care, and ethnic minority children were not over-represented. That said, the authors found improvements were needed in the standard of the residential care that *was* provided for ethnic minority children.

The authorities studied had also made considerable progress towards a workforce which reflects the spread of ethnic groups in the population served. This may not be true for senior management levels nor equally true of all ethnic minority groups, but it is welcome. It will help in fashioning a service sensitive and adapted to the needs of all children. It will help, for example, with a problem this study found that ethnic minority parents do not seek the help of social services as often as white and that ethnic minority children tend to be referred in situations of "crisis".

Much has been achieved but much remains to be done, not least in the use of ethnic origin data and other relevant information by authorities. The authors of this study found a good deal of recording of such data, but precious little evidence of its monitoring or use to inform the management and development of services. There is a clear need here for not just local leadership but national leadership from Government. The Department of Health collects information on children looked after by local authorities and those on the Child Protection Register, but not their ethnic origin. The report has other recommendations for national implementation. However, any serious new commitment must involve a commitment to establish the facts and to stop making policy in the dark.

The research reported here was supported by a grant from the Commission for Racial Equality. The Commission is pleased to have the British Agencies for Adoption and Fostering as its partner in publishing this important study. However, the Commission does not necessarily endorse all the viewpoints expressed in this report.

# Foreword

Felicity Collier, Director, British Agencies for Adoption and Fostering

BAAF welcomes the opportunity to publish this important study commissioned by the CRE and commends it to all responsible for the strategic management of services to children and families, as well as, of course, to social workers and managers, who, on a daily basis, make decisions affecting the lives of individual children.

It is clear that there has been a significant improvement in the five years since the implementation of the Children Act in the quality and appropriateness of the services for black children. However, we cannot be confident even about maintaining current progress – at a time of severe financial constraint, best practice is too often set aside and it is suggested here that there is a disproportionate effect on services to black children and their families. It is of particular concern that so many children are accommodated within two weeks of referral to social services departments and that there are insufficient resources available for preventative work. The speed with which African-Caribbean children move into "care" is very worrying.

This study highlights local authorities' legal responsibility under the Children Act; it also demonstrates the disadvantages experienced by children where there is insufficient priority attached to their ethnic background. It is very timely when considered against the backdrop of public and media attention focused currently on discourses about "political correctness" and the resulting delay said to be experienced by black children awaiting permanent new families. One of the most significant findings of this study is that black children do not "languish" in residential care, but are, in the majority of cases, placed successfully in black families.

However, the study also shows there is no place for complacency. It provides further important evidence in support of critical findings in recent Department of Health Inspections (1995/6) and shows that they have particular implications for children from minority ethnic groups, for example:

- an absence of care plans for 44 per cent of looked after children in particular with relation to mixed parentage children where the figure was 60 per cent and for Asian children 73 per cent;

- little choice in emergency foster placements leading to inappropriate transracial placements and separation of siblings, both of which can lead to long-term drift and dilemmas for all concerned about future moves;

- lack of clear policy and guidance at a strategic level, particularly with regards to the placement needs of children of mixed parentage;

- insufficient priority to providing adequate training and supervision for social workers emphasised in the lack of confidence and practice skills in working with black children and their families.

This study makes important recommendations. It is unacceptable that there continues to be an absence of proper information derived from ethnic monitoring of provision for looked after children on both a national and a local basis. How else can we inform planning for black and white children and address speculation and criticism which continue to be the currency of political debate?

BAAF has had a long-standing commitment to promoting the importance of black children being placed in black families that reflect their particular heritage. We are pleased to see that this is slowly informing social work practice, but much remains to be done.

BAAF wholeheartedly supports the CRE in calling for action now.

*Felicity Collier*

# Introduction

Although Britain is a multiracial and multicultural society, there is much evidence of the failure of public services to adequately address the needs of users from different minority ethnic* groups. This is also true for minority ethnic families and children† who are in contact with social services departments.

For the first time in child care law, the Children Act 1989 placed a statutory duty on local authorities in England and Wales to consider the racial and cultural needs of children who are being looked after by the authority. Section 22(5)(c) of the Act stipulates that when making decisions in respect of children, an authority:

> '... shall give due consideration ... to the child's religious persuasion, racial origin and cultural and linguistic background.'

With the recent implementation of the Children (Scotland) Act 1995, a similar duty has been placed upon local authorities in Scotland, in relation to children in need, looked after children and on courts and adoption agencies when making decisions about adoption.

The Children Act is regarded as a considered piece of legislation based on research evidence about the nature of social services interventions and their impact on children, young people and their families. Much of this research documented the experiences of children in general but little was explained about the circumstances under which children from different ethnic groups came to the attention of social services and their subsequent treatment by these agencies.

Research relating to black children, and undertaken prior to the Children Act, had highlighted several areas of concern, including the high representation of black children within public care, and the failure of social services to adequately meet the needs of black families and children (Bebbington and Miles, 1989; Rowe et al, 1989; Barn, 1993).

Furthermore, research and evaluation of services to black children were greatly hindered by inadequate childcare information systems and continue to be. There are no national statistics on the numbers of black children in the public care system or on Child Protection Registers. Although many authorities have developed local systems which record the ethnic origin of those to whom they provide services, this information is not collected centrally.

## THE AIMS OF THE RESEARCH

Five years after the implementation of the Children Act, it is appropriate to consider how social services departments have responded to Section 22(5)(c) and to ask if there is any evidence of an improvement in social

*\* Throughout this report, the terms minority ethnic and black have been used interchangeably.*

*† Throughout this report, the word "children" refers to children and young people.*

1

work practice with children from diverse ethnic backgrounds. That is the broad purpose of the research study reported here. More specifically, the study has sought to address the nature and pattern of service provision to children from different ethnic groups, including support, accommodation or care by the local authority. Policies, practices and procedures of the local authorities in respect of the Children Act 1989 and the Race Relations Act 1976 have been examined.

## RESEARCH METHODS

This study builds upon earlier work conducted in an inner-city local authority social services department (Barn, 1993). It explores the case histories of 196 children who are either being looked after or supported by three different local authorities. Both black and white young children are included in the sample so that comparisons can be made and any differences or similarities in service provision noted.

An important qualitative dimension has been added through interviews with a sub-sample of this group. In this way it has been possible to include the perceptions of significant individuals – birth parents, foster carers, practitioners, social work managers and the children themselves. Interviews with the senior managers in each of the three authorities have provided important insights into issues of policy and service provision.

## TERMINOLOGY AND DEFINITIONS

Before conducting any research on ethnicity it is important to clarify the terminology to be employed and the way in which data will be classified and analysed.

The Children Act refers to four elements of background – race, culture, religion and language. In this study, quantitative data have been gathered on three dimensions – ethnic origin, religion and first language. Ethnic origin was felt to be an appropriate factor as it recognises diversity, enables identification of particular needs and concerns, and avoids grouping minority ethnic people together as a homogenous mass.

Given the diverse ethnic composition of the authorities in this study, it was important to collect detailed information on ethnic origin, rather than simply broad groupings. Eight main categories have been used: African, African-Caribbean, White European, White other, Asian, mixed parentage, Chinese/Vietnamese, and other. The term "mixed parentage" has been used to reflect the specific experiences of children whose birth parents are from different ethnic origins. In this study, these children had one black and one white parent (in most cases a black father and a white mother).

In presenting the data from this study there are times when it is appropriate to use detailed "ethnic origin" classifications; at other times, because of small numbers, it is appropriate to analyse the data using fewer categories. The four main categories employed are African-Caribbean, Asian, mixed parentage and White. The term "black" is used to refer to minority ethnic groups in general. In the context of the empirical research, it refers to those of African, African-Caribbean, mixed parentage, Asian and Chinese origin. Distinctions of ethnic background are made wherever relevant and necessary in the discussion of our findings.

## THE STRUCTURE OF THE REPORT

The report begins by establishing the current knowledge base on social service provision for black children through a review of the most relevant literature. It also offers a discussion of relevant legislation – the Children Act 1989 and the Race Relations Act 1976. The second chapter provides further details of the aims of the study and the methodology used.

Chapter 3 sets the context for the research by providing a description of the local authorities in which the research was conducted. Information is provided on the ethnic composition of the population within the authorities; the structure of the social services departments (in particular, the teams involved in this research); and the policies of the local authorities relevant to the implementation of Section 22(5)(c) of the Children Act and Section 71 of the Race Relations Act.

Chapter 4 describes the main characteristics of the sample of 196 children. Information is then provided on the needs of the children and their families and the services they received. Where analysis of this information points to major differences between different ethnic groups, these are noted.

The next three chapters address some fundamental issues in good social work practice with black children and their families. Chapter 5 focuses on the assessment of children who are "in need" or who have been referred for reasons of child protection. The placement of the children in the sample is detailed in Chapter 6. Policy, practice and provision are highlighted in these chapters based upon interviews with users and professionals. Chapter 7 explores some positive initiatives, and draws attention to those services which are necessary if local authorities are to take seriously their responsibilities to meet the racial and cultural needs of children and families.

The final chapter of the report draws together the research findings and suggests changes in policy and practice so that "race" and ethnicity are actively addressed in social services provision for children and families.

# Ethnicity, child care and the social services

The general paucity of adequate discussion about the situation of black children in the care system has been highlighted in previous studies (Barn 1990, 1993). Mainstream child care literature, on the whole, has continued to overlook the issue of "race" and by default or design has led to the marginalisation of black children in care.

This chapter offers a glimpse of "race" related child care literature. It is argued that previous research has focused upon limited aspects of the care process, often from a problematic stance, and has failed thereby to document adequately the needs and concerns of black families and children.

The chapter is divided into three sections. The first section discusses the referral and entry patterns of black children and highlights some explanations offered for the disproportionate representation of black children in the care system. The second considers black children's experiences in residential care and in substitute family settings. The final section highlights the existing child care and race relations legislation available to local authority social services departments in England and Wales to address the needs of minority ethnic families and children.

## ENTRY INTO CARE

The referral and entry patterns of black children have received limited attention (Barn, 1990). Much of the literature has concerned itself with the high proportion of black children in care without adequately exploring the issues that have contributed to this.

### Disproportionate representation in the care system

In the absence of national and local authority statistics on the ethnic origin of children in local authority care, research studies have been preoccupied with documenting the disproportionate representation of black children without much explanation as to why they are there (NCH, 1954; Fitzherbert, 1967; Foren and Batta, 1970; Rowe and Lambert, 1973; McCulloch, Smith and Batta, 1979; Lambeth, 1981; Tower Hamlets, 1982). The contribution made by such studies has nevertheless been useful in highlighting this disproportionately high representation.

A group of studies conducted in the Social Services Department of Bradford in the 1960s and 70s by researchers at the University of Bradford showed that black children were more likely to be admitted into care than white children. The first Bradford study to examine admission patterns was carried out between 1966 and 1969 (Foren and Batta, 1970). In defining the "ethnic origin" variable, this study made a simple three category delineation of "white" (white indigenous), "coloured" (African-Caribbean and Asian), and

"Half-coloured" (mixed-parentage). An overwhelming finding of this study was that there was a high rate of reception into care in the mixed-parentage group – over 50 per 1,000 having come into care during the period of the study. The rate of admission for mixed-parentage children was eight and a half times higher than for white children. Moreover, it was found to be even greater for mixed-parentage children under five years old.

A follow up study was conducted six years later (McCulloch, Smith, and Batta, 1979). Data were collected from the official records of Bradford Social Services Department for the year ending 31 March 1975, and these were compared and contrasted with those of the earlier study. The researchers found that mixed-parentage children still had a greater chance of coming into care than either of the other two ethnic groups, that is, "white" and "African-Caribbean and Asians" (109 mixed-parentage children were in care – a rate of 66 per 1000). Mixed-parentage children also came into care at an earlier age and tended to stay in care for longer periods. It was also found that the number of African-Caribbean and Asian children in care had increased much faster than the other two groups since the previous study. A third study which looked at children in care in Bradford Social Services Department came to similar conclusions in terms of its findings on mixed-parentage children (Batta and Mawby, 1981).

Although research studies have pointed to the large numbers of black children in the care system, it is not clear whether black children are, in fact, disproportionately represented. Barn (1993) highlighted the problematic nature of the terms "disproportionate" and "care". She argued that the large numbers of black children in residential homes had often been understood to mean that black children were over-represented in care (NCH, 1954; Lambert, 1970; Rowe and Lambert, 1973; Pearce, 1974; Cawson, 1977). The term "care" had been employed in an ambiguous sense to imply care in general when, in fact, research studies had measured care only by virtue of a child being in a residential institution. Thus children placed in non-institutional settings, for example, foster families had not been included. So, when Rowe and Lambert (1973) asserted that black children spent longer periods in care, it has to be understood that care was used to mean residential care only. Indeed, the figures could be even more alarming if "care" included substitute care in any setting. Whilst it is important to establish "over-representation", it has to be said that high numbers of black children alone should be sufficient to warrant concern about adequate service provision to black families and children.

This over-representation has more recently been documented by other studies (Bebbington and Miles, 1989; Rowe et al, 1989; Barn, 1990, 1993). In her study of almost 600 children, Barn (1993) found that compared with their numbers in the general child population, African-Caribbean and mixed-parentage children were over-represented in the care system. Rowe, Hundleby and Garnet (1989) also found that black children entered the care system in disproportionate numbers compared to their white counterparts. Moreover, they found that African-Caribbean young people were over-represented on entry into care but stayed for brief periods, and that Asian young people were under-represented in the care population.

## Reasons for referral and entry into care

There has been limited research to explain the referral and entry patterns of black children into the care system. While studies have attempted to determine why black children enter care, they have largely overlooked the significance of how families come to be known to the social services in the first instance. Some studies have shown a correlation between length of residence in Britain and knowledge of social services provision (Boss and Homeshaw, 1974; McCulloch and Smith, 1974). It has been argued that Asians are less familiar with service provision due to their more recent settlement. Clearly, such findings hold little meaning in the 1990s. Other factors, such as the inaccessibility and inappropriateness of social service provision, may be more relevant.

Boss and Homeshaw (1974) observed similarities and differences in referral patterns between black and white groups. They found that overall there were few differences in the referrals made, that is, black and white parents were equally likely to refer themselves (45 per cent black, 46 per cent white). Also, similar proportions of black and white cases were referred by other agencies: 40 per cent of the black referrals came from health, education and law enforcement agencies, compared to 39 per cent of the white referrals. Some difference was found when these agencies were singled out; for example, 25 per cent of the black cases were referred by health and education compared to only 16 per cent of the white cases.

About 20 years later, Barn (1993) found that although black parents (primarily African-Caribbean) were equally likely as white parents to refer themselves, there were differences in referrals from statutory agencies. For example, the police and schools were more likely to refer black youngsters for reasons of delinquency than white youngsters. Similarly, black mothers were much more likely to be referred for reasons of mental health by the police and the health service than white mothers. In the light of our knowledge about black youngsters and juvenile justice (Tipler, 1986; Walker, 1988; NACRO, 1989), and black people and mental health (Burke, 1986; Fernando, 1988, 1991), it could be argued that statutory agencies are consciously or unconsciously operating within a racist framework where black families and children are viewed as deviants and as a threat to the moral well-being of society.

There is little systematic account of the circumstances under which black children enter the care system. Explanations have ranged from socio-economic disadvantage (Pinder and Shaw, 1974; CRE, 1977; Lambeth, 1981; Barn, 1993) to family background (Fitzherbert 1967; McCulloch, Smith, and Batta 1979) and institutional and individual racism on the part of the social services (Kornreich, 1973; Pinder, 1982; Johnson, 1986; Barn, 1993). Barn (1993) found socio-economic disadvantage and social workers' negativity to be significant factors in the failure to implement preventative strategies with black families, thereby resulting in the quick disposal of black children into the care system.

## EXPERIENCES IN CARE

### Residential care

As is the case with entry into care, there is a general paucity of information on black children's experiences in the care system. The research in this area is again very patchy and has primarily focused on substitute family placements for black children in care.

In a study of children in long-term care, Rowe and Lambert (1973) found 552 children in their sample group of 2,812 were black, that is, one child in every five. They asserted that in the 28 agencies studied (county, borough, and voluntary bodies in England and Wales, and Scotland) the proportion of black children varied from none to more than 50 per cent. The study showed that black children spent longer periods in institutional care. However, what happens to them while in care has not been researched in depth. Previous research on substitute family placements suggested that black children were more likely to be placed in residential institutions than white children (Raynor, 1969; Rowe and Lambert, 1973; Jackson, 1976; Gill and Jackson, 1983).

Rowe and Lambert (1973) found that in their study of 552 "coloured" children, 164 were in need of a substitute family. The study made little mention of the remaining 388. It is highly likely, since the researchers themselves asserted that 'being of a minority race can be a handicap to substitute family placement', that a majority of the 388 children were confined to residential institutions and that only 164 were deemed to be suitable for substitute family placements. Rowe and Lambert presented their findings in racial terms but only to include that proportion of black children needing substitute families. Their other findings were presented in general terms. Thus although it may have been possible for them to extrapolate other relevant information, they failed to tell us about *black* children's 'length of time in care', 'number of admissions and moves', 'age upon last admission into care', 'number of social workers', 'parental contact', 'legal status', and 'present placement'. It is unfortunate that major national studies such as this have overlooked ethnicity as an important variable.

A disproportionate use of CHEs (Community Home Schools with Education on the premises, formerly known as Approved Schools) for black adolescents was also highlighted by a number of studies in the 1970s (Lambert, 1970; Pearce, 1974; Cawson, 1977). Here a link was drawn between delinquency and CHEs, although a definition of the term "delinquency" was unclear. Lambert (1970) in his study of Birmingham, for example, found that a number of Asian, African-Caribbean, and mixed-parentage children ended up in CHEs simply because of some conflict between themselves and their parents. Pearce (1974) in his study of 125 Community Home Schools concluded:

'West Indian boys have been found to be over-
represented in Community Home Schools, possibly
as a result of differential police activity.'

(Pearce, 1974:323)

The treatment of black children in residential institutions is a much neglected area. A CRE report (1977) stated that the basic needs (for example, skin and hair care, and dietary needs) of black children were not being adequately met, thereby suggesting that if the basic needs were left unmet there was little likelihood of an overall satisfactory situation.

Pinder (1982) in a study of an Observation and Assessment Centre found a situation of great conflict between staff and a group of African-Caribbean "lads". Pinder made links between the management of situations of conflict and the nature and staffing of the establishment which was then a remand home. The study illustrated how staff exercised their position of power:

> *'The typical outcome of the confrontations was a recourse to (further) custodial provision for the lads. From a staff perspective, the following conclusion to a court report . . . exemplifies the logic of these moves in the direction of custody.*
>
> *' "Since returning to Edgefield on 7 July 1978 on a full care order, the less desirable aspects of Hall's character have become more evident, his bullying has increased and when checked for his misdemeanours he blames his colour rather than his behaviour. In separate incidents he attempted to attack one member of staff and struck another in the eye, cutting his eyebrow and causing considerable swelling and discolouration. Since that time his privileges have been withdrawn. It is our opinion that there is little in social services provision to assist this boy and that he best be considered for Borstal training." '*
>
> (Pinder, 1982:13)

Pinder attempted to address the issue of racism but did not discuss the differences between different types of residential institutions. He failed to place the discriminatory treatment of black children in a broader structural context. Nevertheless, his emphasis on practices within the centre and the way these affected the "disposals" of black youth is valuable, and is reinforced by quotes from a deputy officer in charge who talks of black youth as "violent" and as a "clique", and admits that five is the maximum number of black youth the establishment was prepared to take at any one time.

The *Black and In Care* report (1984) mentioned the overt and covert racism experienced by black children in residential institutions. In the first ever conference held for and by black children who were or had been in care, it was emphasised that children had been subject to overt acts of racism. Racist remarks from staff and other white children were common. It was also stressed that staff in these residential homes had little or no knowledge of the experiences of black people in the UK or of black cultures, and therefore racial conflicts between children could not be amicably resolved. The lack of knowledge of black cultures and experiences was perceived to be an inevitable aspect of the negative stereotypes held by white staff. For example, when one young person asked about his culture he was told: 'You don't have to worry about that, you're in England now, and when in

Rome . . .' (*Black and In Care* 1984:24). *Black and In Care* provided an important insight into black children's perceptions of residential institutions.

Barn (1993) found that although the majority of black children in her study were placed in foster families, some use was made of residential institutions, particularly private and voluntary children's homes. The study showed that the experiences of black children varied depending on the nature and location of residential settings. Children placed within their own locality, in residential homes staffed by black and white workers, were able to maintain a healthy sense of their racial and ethnic identity, and good links with their family and the community. Children's homes in rural settings with primarily white staff were alienating for black children and did little to meet their emotional and psychological needs (Barn, 1993).

## Fostering and adoption

Early perspectives on the placement of black children can be effectively positioned within the "colour blind" approach to social work. In the 1960s, the numbers of white babies for adoption decreased; black babies slowly began to be seen as suitable for white couples (Bagley and Young, 1982; Raynor, 1970; Gill and Jackson, 1983). Childless white couples were being offered black babies as a last option. Jackie Kay (1991) poetically articulated the experience of her own adoptive white parents:

> 'The third (agency) liked us
> but they had a five year waiting list.
> I spent six months trying not to look
> at swings nor the front of supermarket trolleys,
> not to think this kid I've wanted could be five.
> The fourth agency was full up.
> The fifth said yes but again no babies.
> Just as we were going out the door I
> said oh you know we don't mind the colour.
> Just like that the waiting was over.'

(Kay, 1991:14)

It was seen as progressive and innovative social work practice to place black babies with white adoptive and foster parents. In the mid 1960s, the British Adoption Project addressed the question: 'Can families be found for coloured Children?' Fifty-three babies of African, Asian, African-Caribbean and mixed parentage background were placed with 51 couples. The vast majority of these families were white. This was seen as a pioneering and radical project which began to break down the barriers which saw black babies as "hard to place". This project was the source of three evaluative studies which assessed the "success" of these transracial placements (Raynor, 1970; Jackson, 1976; Gill and Jackson, 1983). The argument in favour of transracial placements was that black children would otherwise be left to languish in institutions and foster homes (Raynor, 1970; Dale, 1987).

The advocates of transracial adoption pointed to research highlighting reductions in residential services, the difficulty in recruiting and retaining foster carers (Cliffe with Berridge, 1991), and the importance of black children being placed in caring environments whatever the ethnic origin of the carer. They also argued that the notion that black children brought up in white families were emotionally maladjusted was a false one (Tizard and Phoenix, 1993; Gill and Jackson, 1983). Tizard and Phoenix (1993) conducted a study with young people of mixed parentage and concluded that 'having a positive racial identity was not associated with living with a black parent'. Gill and Jackson (1983) regarded 83 per cent of transracial adoptions as successful, based on academic adjustment, self esteem, peer group contact and relationships within the family. Even though Gill and Jackson would point to the relative success of these adoptions, comments such as, 'the children saw themselves as white in all but skin colour', and 'their coping mechanisms are based on denying their racial background' (p137) lead one to question the supposed success of such placements.

In the 1960s and 70s, agencies failed to actively recruit black foster or adoptive carers (Bagley and Young, 1982). At the same time, opponents of transracial placements were beginning to be heard (Small, 1982; Fitzgerald, 1981). The placement of black children in white families began to be highlighted as not just an individual issue (Dean, 1993) but as a political issue which had direct repercussions for the black communities (Divine, 1983; Small, 1984). Hayes (1987) argued that transracial placements led to a dismissal of the possibility of valuing the child's black culture, and Gill and Jackson (1983) acknowledged the damage done to the black community by the removal of black children into white homes.

With the growing recognition of diversity or multiculturalism within British society, social service departments have begun to accept that black children are better placed within black homes. Same race placement has been the next stage of development in the pursuit of identifying a more appropriate placement policy for black children. However, the concept of "same race" and the way it has been interpreted may not be wholly appropriate for all black people. A more individualistic approach, whilst still maintaining the relevance of the political underpinning of the arguments against transracial placements, would be a movement towards racial or ethnic matching (Cheetham, 1982; Smith and Berridge, 1994; Ahmad, 1990). This approach requires a specific matching of a young person's ethnic origins (which incorporates religion and language) with that of any potential carer. This is also a recognition that African or Asian communities are not a homogenous group but reflect a diversity of cultures; differences within these need to be recognised and valued. Barn (1993) found that whilst African-Caribbean children had a reasonably high chance of being placed in an ethnically similar family, the placement needs of other children, namely Asian and Turkish, were not being met to the same degree. The latter tended to be placed in white or African-Caribbean family settings.

# THE LEGAL FRAMEWORK

## The Children Act 1989

The Children Act 1989 was introduced a time when there was growing awareness of the importance of "race" and ethnicity within social work. In relation to looked after children, the Act requires that local authorities *'give due consideration to the child's religious persuasion, racial origin and cultural and linguistic background'* in making decisions about them (Section 22 (5)(c)). Consideration of a child's "race" and ethnicity underpins the basic framework of the Act as important factors in the identification and meeting of need. Reference is made to this basic requirement elsewhere in the Act; for example, in relation to day care, it is stated that childminders and others providing day care should have regard to the child's religious persuasion, racial origin and cultural and linguistic background (Section 74 (6)). Under the Act, a local authority has the power to cancel the registration of any person, who, in the opinion of the authority, is not providing adequate care with respect to the needs of that child. It is evident that the Act has introduced a framework for meeting the needs of children in a holistic manner, and that the racial, religious, cultural, and linguistic needs of children are part of that wider framework.

There has been a considerable amount of Guidance and Regulations issued by the government to accompany the Act (see DoH 1991, vols 1–9). A range of areas from day care to foster and residential placements have been covered. References to issues of "race" and ethnicity are made but remain fragmented and limited in nature. For example, in the guidance on residential care, minimal mention is made of the dietary requirements of minority ethnic children:

> *'Regulation 12 requires that children in homes should be provided with food in adequate quantities properly prepared, wholesome and nutritious and for some reasonable choice to be provided so far as is practicable. Special dietary needs due to health, religious persuasion, racial origin or cultural background must be met.'*

(DoH, *Guidance and Regulations, vol.4, Residential Care,* 1991:25).

In the same volume, in a section on education, an important but brief mention is made of linguistic needs, that is, the need for language tuition where English is not the first language for the child. This fails to make the impact required for this issue to be taken seriously. Similarly, in a section on health, thalassaemia and sickle cell anaemia are given only two lines with reference to staff training and development. Whilst we recognise that issues of "race" and ethnicity are certainly incorporated in the Guidance and Regulations, we think it is important to emphasise the fragmented and minimalist way in which this is done. Moreover, critics have pointed to the vagueness of terms such as 'racial origin, cultural and linguistic background' employed in the Act and accompanying Guidance and Regulations, and view this as 'a watering down of anti-racism' (Stubbs, 1991).

With the Act acknowledging the specifics of work with black children and their families, there has been some attempt made in the literature within this area to reflect the policy changes. *All Equal Under the Act* is a useful tool for social workers who wish to work pro-actively in an empowering way with black families (Macdonald, 1991). It provides an in-depth analysis of discrimination and its manifestation in black people's lives and how workers can use the Act to the benefit of black families. This work goes through the main concepts of the Act highlighting the salient issues regarding "race" and disability. A training pack produced by the Family Rights Group provides useful guidance for trainers to incorporate issues of "race" and ethnicity in any training on the Act (FRG/HMSO, 1991).

Even though the Children Act does contain specific reference to work with black children, Lane (1993) advocated caution to those practitioners who sit back and think it has all been achieved.

> *'Passive acceptance of legislation is likely to have little effect on children's lives. To remove racism from their lives two things are needed: a disproportionate determination to use legislation to ensure the right of every child to equal treatment and a passionate personal commitment to challenge racism wherever it exists, and that means all of us.'*
>
> (Lane, 1993:181)

Although the Act stipulates the consideration of a child's racial, cultural, religious and linguistic background, it is clear that legislation in itself is of limited effect. Positive outcomes will be dependent upon interpretation and implementation of the Act (Ahmad, 1990).

## The Race Relations Act 1976

The Race Relations Act 1976 imposes a duty on local authorities to eliminate racial discrimination and promote equality of opportunity and good race relations (Section 71).

In terms of the work carried out by local authorities, Section 71 refers to two specific areas, namely, employment of staff and service delivery to clients. Research evidence has shown that local authorities have been slow to implement these requirements (CRE, 1978 and 1989).

## Ethnic monitoring

Ethnic monitoring has been advocated as one of the methods which can be used to ensure the effective implementation of the requirements of the Race Relations Act. The collection of such information poses an ethical dilemma for local authorities regarding the best and most appropriate use of such data. Given that there is little factual information about the circumstances of black children looked after by local authorities, there is no doubt that ethnic monitoring would be an effective method to review the numbers of black children being referred to social services. Also, depending on the way the information is collected, it can give the authority an indication of the type of services black children are receiving. Monitoring could also be used to plan future service provision to targeted sections of the community.

An important issue which monitoring will reveal is whether different sections of the black community are excluded, or virtually excluded, from social services' provision. Fewster (1990) highlighted the gaps in provision for Liverpool's 9,000 Chinese population – a group that could be easily ignored because of the stereotypical view that they have close knit communities that look after their own people. The relevance and accessibility of social service provision were also questioned by Jansari (1980) who pointed to similar factors as reasons for the low take-up rate of services by Asian people. Jansari argued that the key to the provision of adequate services to the black communities was the relevance of the service and that this could only be achieved with in-depth knowledge of the different needs of the black communities. Horn (1982) also produced evidence, based on research into Asian families in four social services Area Offices in Bradford, of the low numbers of Asian clients being referred to social services.

In order to fill the gaps in provision of services to the black communities, some local authorities have begun to use ethnic monitoring as a means of assessing the needs of the different black communities. However, ethnic monitoring is not without its critics (Ohri, 1988). Some authorities may believe that with the collection of information on black service users they are carrying out their duty to the black communities, and may see collection of data as a substitute for the improvement of the actual service provision.

It is clear from research conducted by Butt, Gorbach and Ahmad (1994) of the Race Equality Unit of The National Institute of Social Work (NISW) that some authorities have already embarked on ethnic monitoring. Of the 92 responses received from local authorities, 42 had initiated ethnic monitoring and a further 25 were planning to implement ethnic monitoring and record keeping. Ethnic monitoring, however, would not demonstrate the content or quality of the work conducted with black children by social workers. In a review of work with 53 African-Caribbean and other black children, some positive work was highlighted, such as attention to hair and skin care, but the review also revealed clear examples of inappropriate care of black children (Cheetham, 1986). Malahleka and Woolfe (1991) reported on the results of the findings of the British Association of Social Workers' *Action Research Project into Ethnically Sensitive Social Work*, that:

> *'Little change had been achieved in the last ten years, and even more determined efforts must be made to overcome the obstacles which have been shown to lie in the way of ethnically sensitive good practice.'*
>
> (Malahleka and Woolfe, 1991:63)

## SUMMARY

This chapter has documented some of the major issues affecting black children and young people in the care system. The high representation of black children in the care system, and their experiences in residential and foster care have been discussed in the context of the currently available knowledge base.

There is clearly a great dearth of information on the care experiences of black children. While some of the issues have received attention, others have suffered from serious neglect, namely the causes of high representation, the nature and quality of service provision to black families and children, and the variations in these for different ethnic groups. This report begins to address these gaps on the basis of the findings of a new study.

# Methodology

## INTRODUCTION

Addressing the needs arising from the ethnicity of children and their families has been a concern of social services departments for some time. As the discussion in Chapter 1 has indicated, providing appropriate services to children from a wide range of ethnic backgrounds has presented significant challenges to many local authorities. The priority given to raising standards in this area of work has been variable. However, with the passage of the Children Act 1989, for the first time a statutory duty has been placed upon local authorities when making any decision in respect of a child they are looking after to give 'due consideration to the child's religious persuasion, racial origin and cultural and linguistic background' (Section 22(5)(c)).

## AIMS AND OBJECTIVES

To date there is no documentary evidence of the impact of the Children Act on improving social work practice with children from diverse ethnic backgrounds. That is the main focus of this research: to examine the way in which Section 22 (5)(c) of the Children Act is being implemented. More specifically the study has sought to address the following aims:

- to establish the nature and pattern of service provision to children from different ethnic groups, including support, accommodation or care by the local authority;

- to determine any similarities and differences in the services offered by local authorities to children and their families from different ethnic groups;

- to ascertain the perceptions of children, their birth parents, carers and social workers of the services provided;

- to examine the policies of the local authorities in respect of the Children Act 1989 and the Race Relations Act 1976.

The context for the study is the legislative requirement of Section 22(5)(c) of the Children Act and the accompanying Guidance (see Vol.3 para 2.40–2.42). As well as containing specific legislative duties, the Children Act also established clear principles and standards of social work practice that are intended to apply at all times and in all aspects of work with children and young people. Section 22(5)(c) established the principle that an understanding of a child's background, in particularly their ethnicity, must underpin *all* work with children and is not restricted solely to set-piece decision-making occasions.

So it is clear from the above aims that the parameters of the study are broad-based. As well as examining the ways in which social services departments are addressing the needs of the children they are looking after, the research also explores the type of supportive services being offered to children and their families prior to any decision to accommodate.

It was also thought important to conduct a study which focused on both black and white children so that comparisons could be made and any differences or similarities in service provision could be identified.

## RESEARCH METHODOLOGY

To meet the research aims set out above and to ensure that the results have a general relevance to all local authorities, a research project was designed which was both multi-method and multi-site (Robson, 1993). The project had three main components, each involving a different methodological approach:

a) collection of quantitative data from a file study of allocated cases in each of the three authorities;

b) case studies of a sub-group of cases, including interviews with children, their families, carers and social workers;

c) analyses of departmental policies through scrutiny of policy documents and interviews with senior managers.

Each of these methods, discussed more fully below, was useful in addressing particular research objectives. However, the combination of methods was particularly suited to the project overall. First, it enabled the researchers to include macro and micro levels of analysis, examining both the policy and practice context of the social services department and the impact of this on social work with individuals (Bryman, 1988). Secondly, it ensured that the views of those most affected, namely children and their families, were represented. In addition, while the file studies generated sufficient data for the findings to have a general relevance, the case studies offered a fuller understanding of quantitative data.

It was important in researching this topic to adopt an anti-racist, anti-discriminatory approach (Barn, 1994; Humphries and Truman, 1994). The research was designed to not alienate or exclude any minority group. Almost all the interviews undertaken as part of the case studies were conducted by black researchers. This seems to have had positive advantages: it enabled black, and indeed white, respondents to talk openly of practices which they felt to be oppressive and discriminatory; at the same time no white respondents refused to be interviewed because of the ethnic origin of the interviewer.

Our research methodology recognised that much of the previous research on black families had been conducted largely by white researchers, and often from a problematic perspective which pathologised family life (Carby, 1982; Lawrence, 1981). Our focus was to establish the needs and concerns as witnessed not only by the organisations, but also by the families themselves.

## THE THREE RESEARCH AUTHORITIES

In designing the research it was considered important to collect information from more than one site. Local authorities not only serve very different populations, but also have different policy and service development priorities. By gathering data from three very different local authorities, the findings are more likely to be representative of local authorities in general and therefore to have wider applicability.

The three local authorities where the research was conducted included one metropolitan borough, one shire county and a London borough. Throughout this text we refer to these as Metro, County and Borough respectively. The authorities all serve ethnically diverse populations; a more detailed picture of each of the three authorities is provided in the next chapter.

It is worth noting that we received agreement to co-operate in this research from the first three authorities that we approached. All three indicated that this reflected the importance that they attached to issues of ethnicity and culture, together with acknowledgements that they still needed to make progress and that they were very willing to learn.

## THE COMPONENTS OF THE RESEARCH

### The quantitative file study

This component of the research enabled the research team to collate empirical quantitative data on the provision of services and the care experiences of a substantial sample of young people. Because of the nature of the sample, such data cannot provide evidence of whether particular groups of children are over or under-represented amongst those who receive services or are looked after by local authorities. However, and perhaps more importantly, they can indicate whether there are significant differences in the pattern of services provided to young people from different ethnic groups. Where available and relevant to the context, we have added statistical data from the authorities' own monitoring systems and from Department of Health publications.

Data was gathered from the child's file and supplemented where necessary with further information from social work staff. Case files potentially offer a rich source of information. There has, however, been some criticism of the use of case files as a source of research data, since this was not the purpose for which the information had been gathered. In practice, data collection from case files was not straightforward and often had to be supplemented by information known to the social worker but not recorded. However, the greatest problem was the inconsistency and lack of organisation in most files. Retrieving information in such circumstances was a very lengthy process. Any difficulties faced by the researcher in finding essential information from a file are also likely to be faced by other staff who may have occasion to work with the child – the standard of record keeping and the accessibility of relevant information are part of the overall quality of the service provided.

The research sample included all those cases currently allocated to social workers in teams covering defined geographical areas. This provided a sample which included children of all ages, types of legal status, in receipt of a wide range of services and representative of the ethnic composition of users of social services in that area. By analysing all allocated cases it was hoped to include not only looked after children, but also those in receipt of preventative or support services, whether children "in need" or "at risk" and on the Child Protection Register. Details about these children are presented in Chapter 4.

In order to ensure enough numbers of black children in the sample to enable meaningful statistical analysis, we asked each local authority to identify for us those teams with the greatest concentration of children from minority ethnic groups. Additionally, to gain some indication of contrasting experiences, we included a team within County which was outside the city and had a smaller minority ethnic population. In total, seven teams were included in the research: two from Metro, three from County and two from Borough. The actual number of cases in the sample is shown in Table 2.1.

| Local authority | No. of cases |
| --- | --- |
| Metro | 61 |
| Borough | 71 |
| County | 64 |
| Total | 196 |

**Table 2.1**

**Number of cases from each local authority**

The research was conducted over a one-year period between 1994 and 1995.

The quantitative questionnaire was divided into eight major sections:

1. basic information about the child

2. details of most recent referral to social services

3. current services received from social services

4. details of current "looked after" episode

5. child's contact with family

6. information about the child's mother

7. information about the child's father

8. information about the child's social worker

## The qualitative case studies

The quantitative data from the first component was complemented by a qualitative study of a sub-sample of cases. In-depth, semi-structured interviews with a group of children, their parents, carers and social workers, recorded their perspectives on the needs of the children and how well these were being met by social services. The interviews were particularly important in exploring issues around ethnicity and allowing families to express their views on the efforts of social workers and carers to offer appropriate services.

Between 10 and 12 cases were selected in each authority, providing a cross-section by age, ethnic origin, legal status, placement and sex. The researcher then arranged interviews with the significant parties in each case. Children, families and carers were first contacted by the social worker who explained the nature of the research and asked if they were prepared to be interviewed. Not everyone approached was willing to participate. In particular, a disappointingly small number of children were available for interview – sometimes they refused, and at other times either failed to keep appointments or simply changed their minds. On average interviews lasted one hour and were conducted with parents in their own home, with children in places where they felt most comfortable, and with social workers during work time on work premises.

In total, 73 interviews were undertaken during this stage of the research: 18 with children, 14 with birth parents, five with foster carers, four with residential staff and 32 with social workers.

Of the 18 children interviewed, 10 were female and eight male. All four main ethnic groups were represented: four African-Caribbean, seven Asian (including one Vietnamese), five white and two of mixed parentage. There were fairly even numbers of boys and girls within the ethnic groups, except that both children of mixed parentage were female.

When interviewing the birth parents, five interviews were conducted with both mother and father or step-father together, seven were undertaken with the mother alone, and in two instances the father was interviewed on his own. Among the five couples interviewed one was of Asian origin and the other four were white. However, the children of two of the white mothers were of mixed parentage although both mothers currently had white partners. Of the seven mothers interviewed alone three were Asian (including one Vietnamese), three were African-Caribbean and one was white. One of the fathers interviewed was white and the other African-Caribbean.

The sex and ethnic origin of the 32 social workers are shown in Figure 2.1. Just over one third of the social workers were male. In terms of ethnicity, Asian social workers made up the smallest group and African-Caribbeans the largest by a narow margin.

It was only possible to interview the foster carers of five young people: three white female carers (one caring for a child of mixed parentage), one African-Caribbean female carer, and a couple where the mother was white and the father was Maltese. Of the five residential staff interviewed one was a white woman and four were African-Caribbean, equally divided between men and women.

Those interviewed were a very diverse group, able to reflect the full range of issues likely to be faced by both service providers and those children and their families seeking help from social services.

Women

Men

Figure 2.1

Sex and ethnic origin of
social worker interviewees (n)

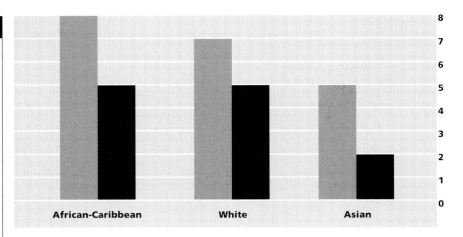

## Policy analysis

The third component was an analysis of the policies and procedures in place in each of the authorities. Copies were requested of any relevant published documentation on both child care services and equal opportunities. In addition, interviews with senior and middle managers explored their views on the application and effectiveness of these policies within their authority. Eleven interviews were undertaken: three in Metro, five in County and three in Borough. The analysis of this material establishes the context for the social work practice recorded in the file study and the qualitative case-related interviews.

## SUMMARY

The over-riding purpose in undertaking this study was to contribute to the development of equitable non-discriminatory services to children. By describing in some detail current social services provision to children from different ethnic groups, we have been able to indicate where progress has been made and to identify examples of good social work practice. Where aspects of policy or practice appear problematic, these too are highlighted. Moreover, by seeking to unpack some of the complexities surrounding this area of work, it is hoped that the research will help local authorities to think through how they can ensure that the services they provide are appropriate and relevant for all the children in their area.

# The local authorities

## INTRODUCTION

In this chapter we describe the three local authorities where the research was conducted. Although the context in which each of these authorities was working was different, the issues with which they were dealing were very similar and will have a resonance for other local authorities.

We start by describing the areas covered by the authorities and the characteristics of their populations; we then focus on the social services departments and the children to whom they provide services; finally we examine the policies in each of the authorities relating generally to equal opportunities in employment and service provision and, more specifically, to the effective implementation of Section 22(5)(c) of the Children Act.

## PEN PICTURES OF THE AUTHORITIES IN THE SAMPLE

### Metro

Metro is an urban, industrial and densely populated area situated in the West Midlands. The borough covers a relatively small area and comprises alternately heavily built up industrialised areas and extensive dereliction. The local authority's Inner Area Urban Programme Team identified some of the many problems facing Metro as:

- high unemployment, particularly long-term joblessness;

- low job creation;

- industrial contraction;

- low service sector workforce;

- mismatch of workforce skills, requiring extensive training programmes;

- poor educational performance in school leavers;

- obsolete transport networks;

- poor council housing and obsolete private housing;

- limited financial resources to tackle these.

Given these problems it is not surprising that in 1981 Metro was in the highest decile – the top ten per cent – of health districts in terms of unemployment, houses lacking a basic amenity, and overcrowded housing.

### County

As a shire county, this authority covers a large geographical area in the Midlands region. The authority area covers a major city and several large market towns surrounded by rural areas. Although overall this is a relatively prosperous county, there are substantial pockets of industrial decay and noticeable material hardship. This is reflected in levels of unemployment which vary from a low of four per cent in the more rural districts to 14 per cent for the city as a whole. However, the inner city areas covered by the social work teams included in this research were then experiencing a level of unemployment of over 21 per cent.

### Borough

Borough is one of the larger inner London boroughs with a population of almost a quarter of a million people. It could be described as a number of villages and towns within a conurbation, each with its own distinctive character, shopping areas and history. One third of households live in rented council accommodation, which is average for all inner London, and almost half (48 per cent) of all households are owner-occupied compared to less than two in five (37 per cent) for inner London as a whole. At the time of the 1991 Census the level of unemployment within Borough was slightly lower than the average for inner London.

## ETHNIC COMPOSITION WITHIN THE THREE AREAS

The 1991 Census is the most comprehensive source of information on the ethnic composition of the population of Britain. Using this census information, Table 3.1 shows the ethnic composition of the total population in England, together with similar information for the population under 18 years of age. This provides the broad multicultural context in which to locate the three authorities.

|  | Total Population | Under 18 Population |
|---|---|---|
| White | 94.0 | 90.0 |
| Asian | 3.5 | 6.0 |
| African/Caribbean | 2.0 | 3.0 |
| Other | 0.5 | 1.0 |
| Total | 100.0 | 100.0 |

**Table 3.1**

**Population by ethnic group: England (%)**

The census information on ethnicity was gathered under 10 headings which can be summarised into four main groups – white, Asian, African/Caribbean, and other.

It is important to note that that the ethnic origin categories available to respondents did not include a specific classification of "mixed parentage". Mixed parentage respondents were asked to classify themselves using an existing ethnic category or to place themselves under the "other" category, with a description of their particular ethnic background:

*'If you are descended from more than one ethnic or racial group, please tick the group to which you consider you belong or tick the*

*"other" box and describe your ancestry in the space provided.'*
*(OPCS, 1991)*

Although this did provide some free-text information, this is not broken down by age nor is it discernible in the published data (Coleman and Salt, 1996). Several research studies have pointed to the large numbers of children of mixed parentage within the public care system (McCulloch, Smith and Batta, 1979; Bebbington and Miles, 1989; Rowe et al, 1989; Barn, 1993); however, the lack of national statistics on children of mixed parentage makes comparative analysis difficult. Such information is important when considering the needs of children receiving social services and hence many social service departments have included clearer information about ethnic background in their own statistics.

Table 3.2 highlights the very different patterns in the composition of the minority ethnic populations of these authorities, even within the very broad categories in which information was available.

| Ethnic origin | Metro | | County | | Borough | |
|---|---|---|---|---|---|---|
| | Total pop. | Child* pop. | Total pop. | Child pop. | Total pop. | Child pop. |
| White | 85.3 | 75.1 | 88.9 | 83.3 | 78.0 | 68.3 |
| Black Caribbean | 2.7 | 2.9 | 0.6 | 0.6 | 10.1 | 11.5 |
| Black African | 0.1 | 0.1 | 0.1 | 0.1 | 3.7 | 5.2 |
| Black Other | 0.5 | 1.4 | 0.3 | 0.7 | 2.5 | 6.0 |
| Indian | 7.9 | 12.7 | 8.4 | 12.0 | 1.2 | 1.4 |
| Pakistani | 1.9 | 4.2 | 0.3 | 0.6 | 0.3 | 0.5 |
| Bangladeshi | 0.8 | 1.9 | 0.2 | 0.5 | 0.3 | 0.6 |
| Chinese | <0.1 | <0.1 | 0.2 | 0.2 | 1.0 | 1.5 |
| Asian Other | 0.2 | 0.3 | 0.4 | 0.6 | 1.3 | 1.6 |
| Other | 0.5 | 1.3 | 0.6 | 1.3 | 1.6 | 3.1 |
| TOTAL | 100.0 | 100.0 | 100.0 | 100.0 | 100.0 | 100.0 |

**Table 3.2**

**Population by ethnic group: study local authorities (%)**

* "Child" refers to children and young people under the age of 18.
*Source: 1991 Census*

## Metro

In Metro, minority ethnic groups make up 15 per cent of the total population, and 25 per cent of the child population, as shown in Table 3.2 above. These proportions are summarised into four main groups – white, black, Asian and other as presented above. This places Metro within the top decile of authorities in terms of the proportion of the population that is from minority ethnic groups. The largest minority ethnic group consists of those who describe their origin as Indian and make up 54 per cent of the ethnic population of the borough. The second largest group is black Caribbean. Within the child population "Indian" is also the largest group followed by "Pakistani".

### County

The minority ethnic population of County is not distributed evenly across the authority; the highest concentration is in the city and one of the larger towns. This needs to be borne in mind when using authority-wide statistics for comparative purposes. In County, 11 per cent of the population is from minority ethnic groups which is high in comparison with the overall figure for the region of five per cent. Details of the distribution of population by ethnic group are shown in Table 3.2.

The figures in Table 3.2 are for the whole County area. However, the proportion of the population of the city which comes from minority ethnic groups is significantly higher at 28.5 per cent. Outside London, this city is the local authority area with the highest percentage of people from minority ethnic groups. Most are of Asian origin, with many having come to Britain from East Africa – three quarters of the minority ethnic population describe themselves as "Indian". The areas covered by the social work teams in this research became home to the majority of minority ethnic groups who settled in the city; here the proportion of the child population under 16 who are from minority ethnic groups is 60 per cent overall.

### Borough

In Borough just under a quarter (22 per cent) of the population is from minority ethnic groups; this compares with an average figure of 26 per cent for all inner London boroughs. Borough has a much smaller Asian population than inner London as a whole; a difference that is even more marked in the child population. The detailed figures given in this table point to the greater diversity in Borough's population, as indicated by the relatively high numbers of people who wished to classify themselves in the "other" categories – "Black other", "Asian other", and "other". Local information suggests that this refers to the substantial Vietnamese and Turkish communities in Borough. The high numbers in the "Black other" category, particularly in the child population, refer to people who regard themselves as "Black British", or of "mixed parentage", reflecting the established nature of the black community in this area.

## SOCIAL SERVICES DEPARTMENTS

Having drawn an outline of the three authorities and their populations, we focus now on the social services departments and the social work teams that participated in this research. As we have noted, the characteristics of these three authorities were very different; however, they all shared an overriding concern with trying to deliver good quality services within tightening budget constraints. It was apparent from interviews that when faced with reduced resources, senior managers concerned themselves with the maintenance of good standards and the survival of existing child care services.

## Metro

This authority, like many others, had just completed a reorganisation from generic teams to specialist children and family teams and adult teams. The greater emphasis given to Community Care meant that the authority was slow in implementing the Children Act. The recent reorganisation of the department had meant not only major shifts in personnel, but also a change in the focus of service delivery and the catchment areas of the two teams participating in the research. Looked at more closely, there were major differences between the two teams.

Team M1 had a stable and consistent staff group with both a manager and principal social worker who had been in post for a considerable time. The team consisted of two managers, six social workers, one assistant social worker and one welfare rights worker. Two social workers had been in post for over five years with the authority, gaining considerable experience of child protection work and practice teaching. The workers had regular supervision and team meetings on a monthly basis. This team would regularly help out neighbouring teams which were experiencing staff shortages. Both managers within this team were white; of the six social workers four were African-Caribbean, one was Asian and one was white.

Team M2 serviced some of the authority's most deprived wards. Demands on the services provided by this team seriously stretched its available resources; 37 cases allocated to this team remained unallocated at the time of the research. The team consisted of one manager (no principal was in post at the time), three full-time permanent social workers, one part-time social worker, one assistant social worker, two agency workers and one translator. Before field work on the research was completed, all three of the full-time permanent workers had left or were in the process of leaving. The manager and social workers were under considerable pressure to prevent the team from being submerged by the volume of work. There was a perception within the team that a lack of forward planning and lengthy recruitment processes had contributed significantly to their problems. The ethnic composition of Team M2 was six African-Caribbean (including the manager), one Asian, and two white workers.

## County

Social Services in County were organised on a geographical basis, with the authority divided into four divisions. Although the majority of services were delivered through these geographical divisions, there was also a fifth division responsible for services across the county. For instance, children's residential services and other specialist children's services were provided by this county-wide division.

Three area teams from County participated in the research; two neighbouring inner city teams and one team covering one of the larger towns in County. The two teams from the city area, C1 and C2, were within one division, the third team, C3, from another. Although C1 and C2 served neighbouring parts of the city, there were significant differences in their populations. For instance, C2 had the more diverse population with a higher proportion of African and African-Caribbean people (8.8 per cent). In contrast, C1 had the highest proportion of people of Indian origin, making up two thirds of the total population.

The team leaders from C1 and C2 were both black – one of mixed white/Caribbean origin, one Asian – and the leader of C3 was white. At the time of the field work, C1 had a complement of seven workers in addition to the team leader – three of them were Asian, and four white, and a black (mixed parentage) student on placement. C2 had six full-time and one part-time social workers: one Asian, two African-Caribbean, and the rest white. In C3, which served the more rural area, the team was made up of five full-time and two part-time social workers and a family support worker. In this group there was one Asian and one African-Caribbean full-time social worker, the rest were white.

### Borough

Borough was organised on a purchaser/provider split. Social work assessment and support was offered through eight geographical Children and Families Teams together with a hospital-based social work team. Additional support was available through early years services, the Adolescent Resource Centre, and the Care to Community team supporting young people leaving care.

Two social work teams participated in the research. Both team leaders were male, one African-Caribbean and one white. B1 comprised seven social workers, three African-Caribbean and four white, together with 1 Asian benefit support worker. Of the 10 social workers in B2, six were African-Caribbean and two each Asian and white.

## THE POLICIES OF THE LOCAL AUTHORITIES

One of the aims of this research was to examine the policies of the local authorities particularly in relation to implementing Section 22(5)(c) of the Children Act of 1989 and Section 71 of the Race Relations Act of 1976. In fulfilment of this aim we scrutinised relevant policy documents from each of the authorities and conducted interviews with middle and senior managers. Below we review those policies and the ways in which they were implemented; the policies are analysed in later chapters.

### Equal opportunities policies

All three authorities had equal opportunities policies in respect of both employment and service provision. In addition, each of the authorities at various times had introduced initiatives to strengthen or promote these (for example, Black workers groups, extensive use of exemptions under the Race Relations Act*, Race Equality Groups). The general picture was one where authorities had tried hard to operate in an equitable fashion, while recognising that this goal still had to be achieved. This perception applied to both equal opportunity in employment and in the provision of services.

*Section 5(2)(d) of the Race Relations Act 1976 permits organisations offering personal welfare services to recruit staff from partucular ethnic groups if these services can most effectively be provided by a person from a particular ethnic group.*

One measure of equal opportunities in employment is the extent to which the ethnic composition of the workforce reflects the local population. This demonstrates fairer employment practices, and is important because it increases the likelihood that service users will also be treated equitably and in a less discriminatory manner. In all three authorities a growing proportion of professional staff was from minority ethnic groups; there was, however, a disproportionately low number of black staff within senior management. For instance, in County, 11 per cent of all social services staff were black (ranging from two to 25 per cent from more rural to the city divisions), eight per cent of middle managers were black, but the senior management team was all white. So the opportunities for generating the greater cultural awareness that a multicultural staff group could bring to service delivery had not been realised in policy formation and strategic management.

Each of the authorities also had policies or equality statements which declared their values in relation to services for children from different ethnic groups. These were included in different ways in each of the authority's Children's Services Plans. For instance, Metro and County included specific sections on black children which identified future action points, and Borough had a comprehensive policy statement, *Equality for children and their families*. Some extracts are provided below:

*'The needs of black children require special attention and include promoting their identity within their own culture, promoting knowledge and understanding of their culture among white staff, and encouraging the recruitment of black child care staff, foster parents and adopters.'*

(Metro)

*'Prejudice and discrimination of all kinds are an everyday reality in many children's lives. Services provided by the local authority should seek to promote and encourage a positive self image.'*

(County)

*'All children and their families are entitled to equal access to services which do not discriminate on grounds of religion, ethnic origin, linguistic background, culture, gender, disability or sexual orientation. However, this does not mean that all children and their families will receive an identical service but rather that services will recognise and respect their particular differences and meet their particular needs.*

*'No child . . . should be refused a service or receive a diminished service because services are not designed to meet their particular needs. The service should be changed as a matter of urgency to meet their needs.'*

(Borough)

## Equal opportunities training

All authorities were clear about their policies towards children from different ethnic groups; how these were manifested in practice will become more evident in subsequent chapters. One possible mechanism to enhance standards in meeting policy objectives is training, for instance, race awareness training or anti-discrimination training. At the time this research was carried out, all three authorities were rethinking their approach to such training.

In interviews, managers identified a series of questions which had arisen for the departments. These are summarised below:

- Should training be a broad programme for all staff members, or should it be more targeted?

- Should all training courses contain a component on working with black clients?

- Were focused training events, such as those on black children in the care system, more relevant?

- What was the most effective form of race equality training? What balance was required between race awareness and more challenging training on anti-discriminatory practice?

- What was the best way to meet the needs of new staff and to update the skills of existing staff?

- Was anti-racist training better done within teams, or as part of skills development for individuals and teams?

These departments, like many others, had put resources into race-awareness training in the 1980s. However, the momentum had since been lost and a clear or strategic approach to race equality training was lacking in all three authorities. For instance, in the past, Borough had a strong reputation as an authority that gave high priority to equal opportunities, but training in this area had since dropped down on the agenda. As a consequence the department was failing to meet the needs of new staff or develop a more sophisticated approach based upon an awareness of "race" and ethnicity.

There was also some re-thinking of the best way to provide such training. One manager saw it thus:

> 'A one or two-day training session (anti-racist, anti-discrimination) isn't going to help anyone. I would argue that what is needed is training at a team level – developing practice and developing staff – so that when they work with black families the basic knowledge exists and is a foundation to work from. It is not about management leading on this; in my team I get staff to lead so that there is a shared ownership. As a team we have developed over the past two to two-and-a-half years to the extent that any one of my team could do a very good assessment on a black family.'

(Black Area Manager, County)

## Placement policies

For looked after children, finding an appropriate placement is pivotal in meeting the needs of the child. In seeking to address needs around ethnicity, many authorities have adopted placement policies in respect of children and young people from minority ethnic groups. However, it has often been noted that staff in social services departments are not always aware of departmental policies, or they may believe that a certain policy operates when, in fact, this is not the case (DHSS, 1985; SSI, 1990).

This was evident in the three local authorities surveyed in relation to placement policies. There was a tendency for team leaders and service managers to assume their local authority had agreed a fairly blanket policy of "same race placement", while senior managers were more inclined to be pragmatic in their approach. No written policies were available with respect to the placement needs of minority ethnic children.

*'There is no placement policy within the authority. This is a deliberate choice because quite honestly it would be pointless at present because we could never meet it . . . The prospects of sophisticated matching on race and culture, religion and language is a luxury we just don't have.'*

(White Senior Manager, Borough)

*'We follow the DoH line, which is that a number of factors are taken into account and an appropriate match is only one of these. We seek it (appropriate match) where it is feasible, but we wouldn't not place a child because a same-race placement was not available.'*

(White Senior Manager, County)

*'You have to make a decision based on the needs of the individual young person and that underpins the whole (same race placement) policy . . . I think we have worked quite hard to make sure we have got a policy which means something and isn't just tokenistic and which can be ignored . . . but it is also important that it isn't so incredibly rigid that you end up forgetting about the individuals in the middle.'*

(White Senior Manager, Metro)

Whatever the formal position or official policy, the staff in the authorities surveyed had a shared understanding about the importance of ethnicity in placing a child. They started from a presumption that, other things being equal, a child was best placed with a family that most nearly matched his or her own ethnic background. While this policy was most important for black children it was also true for white children. In authorities with increasing numbers of foster carers from diverse communities, a shortage of carers may make "matched" placements difficult for both black and white children.

In Chapter 6 we consider how effectively this policy or understanding operated in practice and the issues that this raises for social workers and their managers.

## Allocation policies

The criterion for selecting the sample in this research was that each case should currently have an allocated social worker, ensuring that as well as looked after children, the sample would include children on the Child Protection Register (CPR) and other groups identified as "children in need". Every Children's Services Plan contains priority lists of those children likely to be children in need, although this is not linked to any commitment to allocate social workers. We were therefore interested in whether the departments had policies, either implicit or explicit, on the allocation of cases to social workers.

All authorities agreed that children on the Register were the first priority for allocation to a social worker – a priority largely determined because of the monitoring of unallocated CPR cases by the Social Services Inspectorate – followed by looked after children. The availability of resources was a major consideration for groups other than these.

The three authorities had very different capacities to allocate staff. Metro had difficulties in ensuring that all children on the Register had an allocated worker, largely due to the imbalances in team workloads which were noted earlier. In Borough few social workers were able to undertake preventative work, although a recent review by auditors had suggested that average case loads could be increased, thereby enabling more preventative work to be undertaken. The case loads of the teams in County included a surprisingly high proportion of "children in need" cases, about 30 per cent of the total.

We also asked whether departments had any written policy or implicit understanding about matching the ethnicity of the allocated worker with that of the child needing placement. None of the authorities had an explicit policy on this although some staff mentioned a broad understanding that, if possible, black workers would be allocated to work with black users. It was recognised that this was a complex issue where several factors had to be taken into account, quite apart from the practicalities of trying to implement such a policy. Many of those interviewed cautioned against such a policy for several reasons:

- black workers did not necessarily want to specialise in this way;

- the danger of allowing white workers to opt out of developing the skills to provide an appropriate service to users from black and minority ethnic groups;

- some users did not want a worker who might have connections with their own community. Such concerns about confidentiality seemed to undermine black workers' professionalism.

Practice was informed by balancing two principles: a belief that *all* workers, regardless of their ethnicity, should be capable of providing a service to any client and that they should provide the best available service to meet the particular needs of each user.

*'Any person should be capable of working with a range of families, but where there is a particular cultural issue it may be better for a worker from that background to deal with it.'*

*'Sometimes black workers can work more effectively with black families . . . not in every case, but in some cases where cultural issues are inextricably woven into the reasons for the family requiring a service. In those cases, a worker who shares the family's heritage would be the only person who can assess them properly.'*

Each of the three authorities served multicultural communities with substantial proportions of the population from diverse ethnic backgrounds. It is therefore to be expected that they would develop policies which expressed their commitment to equal opportunities in terms of service delivery and employment. However, policies still need to be translated into practice. As one Team Leader noted:

*'I think the policies are fine, but at the end of the day I think the policies are as good as the people who implement them . . . ultimately it is down to those people in positions of power who appoint people and who allocate work to people.'*

In the next three chapters, we examine more closely the impact of these policies on the services offered to almost 200 children who sought help from these departments.

## SUMMARY

- While the three local authorities used as research sites were different, taken together they reflected a general picture of the policies and practices of social services departments.

- The organisational structures of the authorities were different; for instance, Metro had only recently moved from generic to Children and Family Teams, County had a geographical structure, and Borough had adopted a purchaser/provider split for children's services.

- The seven social work teams which participated in the research were broadly representative in ethnicity of the populations they served: overall about 45 per cent of the staff were African-Caribbean, 35 per cent were white, and 20 per cent were Asian.

- All three authorities had equal opportunities policies in respect of both employment and service provision. The Children's Services Plan within each local authority made mention of the needs of black children.

- While each of the authorities had, in the past, devoted resources to equal opportunities training, all three were currently debating the most appropriate way forward.

- Although most of the social workers interviewed assumed that their authority operated a clear "same-race" placement policy, there were no written policies to this effect and senior managers implemented policy in this area in a less "blanket" fashion.

- There was a clear hierarchy for the allocation of different cases to social workers: child protection cases were accorded the highest priority, followed by looked after children and then children in need. Borough had problems even in allocating workers to all child protection cases; only County was able to allocate social workers to "children in need" with any consistency.

- None of the authorities operated a policy of "matching" family and social worker on ethnic grounds; ethnicity was taken into account alongside other factors on a case by case basis.

# The families and children –
# A profile

## INTRODUCTION

This chapter explores the case histories of two groups of children, namely those who were looked after by the authorities and those in receipt of support services but living at home with their families. It also provides background information on the 196 children whose cases were studied.

## THE SAMPLE

The sample included 61 children from Metro, 71 children from Borough, and 64 from County. The figure below shows the numbers of looked after children and those in receipt of help and assistance from the social services.

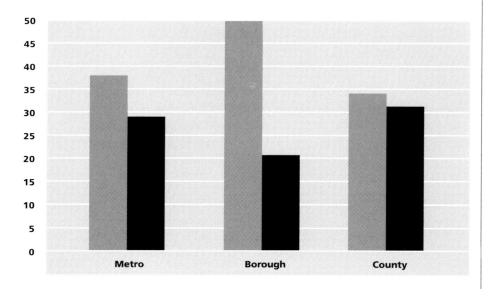

**Figure 4.1**

**The sample:
Distribution of looked after
and support cases (n)**

## ETHNIC BACKGROUNDS OF CHILDREN

Our sample of 196 children comprised six ethnic groups: Figure 4.2 shows the proportions of each ethnic group included in the study.

Nearly half the children in the sample were white. The three predominant minority ethnic groups were African-Caribbean (18 per cent), Asian (14 per cent), and mixed parentage (16 per cent).

Interestingly, only two of the three local authorities (Metro and County) had allocated cases of Asian families and children. Whilst Borough had no

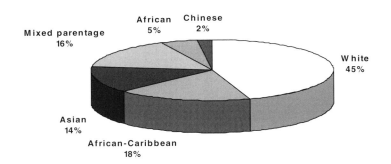

**Figure 4.2**

**Distribution of ethnic groups:
total sample (%)**

allocated cases of Asian families and children, a small number of Chinese
families and children were found to be involved with the social services.

|  | Metro % | Borough % | County % |
|---|---|---|---|
| White | 39 | 44 | 50 |
| African-Caribbean | 21 | 29 | 3 |
| Asian | 16 | 0 | 28 |
| Mixed parentage | 23 | 10 | 16 |
| Chinese | 0 | 4 | 2 |
| African | 0 | 13 | 2 |
| Total | 100 | 100 | 100 |

**Table 4.1**

**Local authority variation –
children in total research sample
(%)**

## Children of mixed parentage

Children of mixed parentage were a significant group in the sample. It was
notable that most such children had a white birth mother. Of the 30 mixed
parentage children about whom information was available, 27 had a white
mother, two had a mixed parentage mother and one had an African-
Caribbean mother. Of the 22 black fathers, 11 were African-Caribbean, five
Asian, three African, and three of mixed parentage.

This confirms previous research by Barn (1993) whose study of a social services
department in a London borough found that the vast majority of looked after
children of mixed parentage had a white mother and a black father.

An analysis of census data also suggested that 'inter-ethnic unions are
generally more common among ethnic minority men than among ethnic
minority women' (Coleman and Salt, 1996). For example, according to the
1991 census figures, 39.5 per cent of African-Caribbean men aged 16–34
were married or cohabiting with white women, compared with 20.9 per cent

of African-Caribbean women of the same age married or cohabiting with white men. Whilst this may partly account for the numbers of children from this type of mixed union (that is, white mother/black father), it is still not clear why these families might face greater difficulties than families with a black mother/white father. A preliminary discussion of this phenomenon is offered elsewhere (Barn, forthcoming).

## GENERAL CHARACTERISTICS OF THE SAMPLE

### Family structure

The vast majority of the children and young people in the sample were from one-parent and nuclear family structures (47 per cent and 39 per cent respectively). Whilst some children may have had wider family networks, only a small minority of each ethnic group was actually residing within an extended family. There was little evidence to support the common stereotype of Asian families living in extended households: only three of the 28 Asian children were living in extended families.

The biggest group of children who came from a single-parent family were African-Caribbean (61 per cent), followed by those of mixed parentage (51 per cent), white (43 per cent), and Asian (25 per cent). The numbers of Chinese and African children were small in comparison with other groups. However, it should be noted that eight of the ten African children came from single-parent families.

Of the married mothers who were separated or divorced, the majority were white. Almost a fifth of the white mothers whose marriage had ended had been in a mixed marriage.

We found that a significant number of Asian mothers were single as a result of separation/divorce or widowhood.

### Age

Less than a quarter of the children in the sample were under the age of five (22 per cent). The majority of the children were adolescents (13 and above) (44 per cent), followed by those between the ages of 6–12 (34 per cent).

Although there were no significant differences between ethnic groups, it was found that African-Caribbean and mixed-parentage children were more likely to be represented in the adolescent group than other children (54 per cent and 52 per cent respectively compared with 41 per cent of whites and 36 per cent of Asians).

Among the under-fives, we found no differences between white, Asian, and mixed parentage proportions. The number of African-Caribbean under-fives, however, was significantly lower than these other groups.

There were only four Chinese children in the sample. Of these, two were under five and two were adolescents.

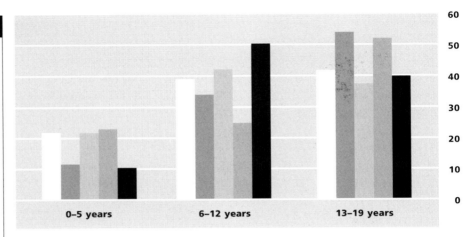

White

African-Caribbean

Asian

Mixed parentage

African

**Figure 4.3**
**Age by ethnic group (%)**

### Sex

The sample included 105 girls (54 per cent), and 91 boys (46 per cent).

### Place of birth

Almost all the children had been born and brought up in Britain (92 per cent). Of those born outside Britain, eight were born in Africa, four in the Caribbean, two in the Indian sub-continent, and two elsewhere.

### Language

English was the first language for over three quarters of children and families (79 per cent). For the 28 Asian children and families in the sample, Punjabi (50 per cent) and Gujarati (39 per cent) were the other two major languages spoken.

### Religion

Of the 196 cases in total, religion had been recorded for only 102. Thus, in almost half the cases, no information was known about the child and family's religious background. Interestingly, religious background information had been recorded for all 28 Asian children and their families: Sikh (43 per cent), Muslim (32 per cent), and Hindu (25 per cent).

### Disability

The great majority of children – 161 – had no disability (82 per cent). Learning disability was the major disability recorded (16 per cent), followed by physical disability (two per cent) and visual impairment (one per cent).

Two per cent of children with disabilities experienced disability as a result of sickle cell anaemia, one per cent as a result of HIV infection.

### Parental country of birth

#### Mother

All the white mothers were British born. All the Asian mothers were from the Indian-subcontinent or Africa; the vast majority were from the former. Of the African-Caribbean mothers, 65 per cent were from the Caribbean, the remainder were born in Britain. No African or Chinese mother was British-born.

### Father

Information was only available about 108 fathers compared with 165 mothers. Of these, all the white fathers were born in Britain. Of the Asian fathers, the majority were from the Indian sub-continent, four were from Africa and five were born in Britain. Information was only available about six African-Caribbean fathers all of whom were born in the Caribbean.

Of those who were fathers to children of mixed parentage, eight were born in Britain, four in the Caribbean, and two in Africa.

## Parents' age

### Mother

Information was available for 151 cases. Of these, the majority were women over the age of 25. Almost fifty per cent were between the age 25–35 and 32 per cent were between the age of 36–45 years. Only a very small proportion of the children came from families where the mother was over the age of 45 (three per cent); while 16 per cent came from families where the mother was under the age of 25.

### Father

Information was only available for 85 cases. In comparison with mothers, there were more fathers over the age of 45 (18 per cent compared to three per cent of women), and fewer fathers under the age of 25 (11 per cent compared to 16 per cent women). The majority of the children came from families where the father was between the ages of 25–45.

## Socio-economic background

### Housing

Information related to housing was available in only 84 cases, that is, for only 43 per cent of the sample. We found that the majority of youngsters came from households where the family lived in local authority accommodation.

### Parental employment

Seventy-two per cent of the mothers and 57 per cent of the fathers were unemployed. Larger numbers of white mothers were found to be unemployed (80 per cent) compared with African-Caribbean (60 per cent) and Asian mothers (55 per cent).

## PROCESS OF REFERRAL

### Sources of referral

There were four major referral agencies – police (14 per cent), schools (18 per cent), health service (16 per cent) and parents (20 per cent). Referrals by other local authorities also featured significantly (16 per cent), particularly in the London and shire authorities. This indicates a geographical mobility of families which was usually within the same area.

The study revealed an interesting aspect of the process of referral: while white parents made self-referrals to the social services agencies for help and support, black parents were more likely to be referred by a statutory agency. The two largest groups of black parents represented in the sample were African-Caribbean and Asian. Families of mixed parentage children were most likely, of all groups, to seek the help of social services (see Table 4.2); the majority of such referrals came from white mothers.

Where referrals had been made by statutory agencies (namely police, education and health authorities), Asian children and families were most significantly represented (71 per cent) compared with African-Caribbean (50 per cent), white (43 per cent) and mixed parentage (37 per cent) children.

The low self-referral of black parents requires attention by the local authorities and raises some important questions.

- Do black parents perceive social services as catering for white clients only?

- Are they dissuaded by the negative experiences of other black people?

- What efforts have social services made to welcome black families and children?

- Are black parents still unaware of the help and assistance which social services can give?

Local authorities need to examine their efforts to publicise services to all sections of the community, and also to explore the relevance and appropriateness of their services for all sections of the community.

**Reasons for referral**

Some of the major reasons for which families were referred to the attention of the social services appeared to relate to child protection, for example, suspected child abuse (41 per cent) or parental neglect (26 per cent). The criterion of "allocated cases" employed in our research sample probably explains this situation. Because of the high priority given to child protection cases, cases likely to be allocated to a social worker were those where there were child protection concerns (see Chapter 3).

The majority of referals of African-Caribbean and Asian families and children were from statutory agencies such as health, education and the police, and in the area of child protection (suspected child abuse, parental neglect and mother's mental health). In these situations, the families did not themselves choose to seek the help of social services, but were referred by other agencies concerned about the welfare of children. Three of the four

| Ethnic group | Self-referral % | Statutory referral % |
| --- | --- | --- |
| African-Caribbean | 15 | 50 |
| Asian | 4 | 71 |
| Mixed parentage | 33 | 37 |
| White | 26 | 43 |

Table 4.2
Referrals by ethnic group (%)

Chinese children had been referred for child protection reasons whilst the fourth had been abandoned and was reported to have no carer although his mother was traced at a later date. No definite pattern could be identified for the ten African children in the sample for whom the reasons of referral were extremely varied. White children and those of mixed parentage were likely to be referred because of neglect, suspected child abuse and children being beyond parental control. Also, "suspected child abuse" was more likely to be a factor in the referral of white children than black (16 per cent and six per cent respectively).

What, however, are we to make of the reasons for referral for African-Caribbean and Asian families? We can see that Asian children were represented significantly in the "suspected child abuse" category, and both Asian and African-Caribbean children were highly represented where there were concerns about a parent's (usually mother's) mental health.

It is important to recognise that our data refer to a relatively small group of families. Indeed, there were only 28 children of Asian origin in a group of almost 200 allocated cases. It would therefore be unwise to form generalisations from such small numbers. A much larger sample would be needed to establish some definite patterns of referrals, and the concomitant problems and needs. A study of all referrals in a given period of time would be required to measure the level of incidence of child abuse and neglect.

Analysis of this study needs to be placed in the overall total context of actual numbers if it is to be of significance. Given the small sample, we can still explore the circumstances of these families and social services' practices and procedures. It would appear that the ways in which information was recorded at the point of referral (presenting problem) and subsequent case recording had a significant impact upon the process of assessment and intervention. This is discussed further in the following chapter.

Although issues of "race" and ethnicity have been given some attention within the social services in the last two decades, understanding and appreciation of different cultural norms, values and traditions are still at an embryonic stage and often located within a Eurocentric framework (Ahmed, 1986; Dominelli, 1988; Ahmed, 1990). Cultural differences in child rearing and discipline are subject to misinterpretation and misunderstanding. For example, a young Asian woman in conflict with her parents may be

| Reasons | African-Caribbean | Asian | Mixed parentage | White |
|---|---|---|---|---|
| Parental neglect | 9 (26%) | 3 (11%) | 8 (26%) | 28 (32%) |
| Suspected child abuse | 10 (29%) | 21 (75%) | 12 (38%) | 33 (37%) |
| Suspected child sexual abuse | 2 (6%) | 2 (7%) | 2 (6%) | 14 (16%) |
| Parents' mental health | 11 (31%) | 9 (32%) | 6 (19%) | 7 (8%) |
| Beyond parental control | 4 (11%) | 4 (14%) | 8 (25%) | 24 (28%) |
| Delinquency | 2 (6%) | 4 (14%) | 4 (13%) | 12 (14%) |
| Non-attendance at school | 1 (3%) | 2 (7%) | 3 (10%) | 12 (14%) |
| Request of child | 4 (11%) | 2 (7%) | 0 (0%) | 3 (3%) |
| Total (n) | 35 | 28 | 31 | 87 |

**Table 4.3**

**Reasons for referral to social services by ethnic origin of child (n and %)\***

Note: Due to the multiplicity of reasons which could be recorded, numbers given do not add up to the actual total for each ethnic group.

perceived by those in authority (such as police and/or school) to be in need of protection. This definition of the "presenting problem" then becomes the basis for social work assessment and intervention. Thus it is not simply a matter of recording the reasons for referral; such reasons are linked to the power base of the referral agent and carry a great deal of weight in subsequent investigations and the treatment the child experiences.

Children caught up in situations of domestic violence can also be at risk of abuse and neglect. Certainly for some of the Asian children in our sample, there were issues resulting from domestic violence, high stress levels for mothers with violent partners, and concerns about the mother's mental health. In such situations, the welfare of the child is of paramount importance for social services. Support services for families in these situations are worthy of exploration, otherwise merely acknowledging the child protection issues, perhaps by registration onto the Child Protection Register, could compound the problems suffered by the child. Issues around child protection and support services are discussed in the following chapter.

## ALLOCATED SOCIAL WORKERS

### Ethnic background

All three local authorities had made efforts to recruit black workers, particularly African-Caribbean. Indeed, 39 per cent of the sample had an African-Caribbean worker, while 44 per cent had a white worker and 17 per cent had an Asian worker.

This study found that minority ethnic and white children and families were able to receive a service from social workers from different ethnic backgrounds. It is interesting to note that while African-Caribbean children and families were most likely to be allocated a social worker from a similar background, this was not the case for other minority ethnic children.

| Ethnic origin of child | Ethnic origin of Social Worker | | | |
|---|---|---|---|---|
| | African-Caribbean (%) | Asian (%) | White (%) | Total (n) |
| African | 90 | 10 | 0 | 9 |
| African-Caribbean | 78 | 0 | 22 | 32 |
| Asian | 0 | 46 | 54 | 26 |
| Mixed-parentage | 39 | 13 | 48 | 31 |
| Chinese | 50 | 25 | 25 | 4 |
| White | 28 | 17 | 55 | 82 |

Table 4.4

Ethnicity of allocated social worker

## Sex

Almost three-quarters of the sample were allocated a female social worker. Although our interview sample includes a more balanced mix of male and female social workers, it is clear that the great majority of social work practitioners are female.

## SUMMARY

This chapter profiles the families and children who came to the social services departments for help and assistance.

- African-Caribbean (18 per cent), mixed parentage (16 per cent) and Asian (14 per cent) children were equally well represented in our sample.

- To meet the requirements of Section 22 (5) (c) of the 1989 Children Act, it is important that information is recorded systematically about the child and family's racial, cultural, religious and linguistic background. Our study shows that while information about the child's ethnic origin was usually available, other data was difficult to ascertain. Indeed, information about religious background had only been recorded for 50 per cent of the sample.

- Almost half the sample came from one-parent families. The pressures of bringing up children require consideration so that appropriate help and support can be provided.

- Information about fathers was extremely sketchy. It is important that social services record such data which could provide useful information for the child particularly when parental contact is lost.

- The low self-referral rate of Asian and African-Caribbean families was found to be significantly different from those for white children and children of mixed parentage (who were mainly referred by their white mothers).

- Some of the major reasons for which families were referred to the attention of the social services appeared to be in the area of child protection, for example, suspected child abuse (41 per cent) and parental neglect (26 per cent).

- The reasons given for referral varied for different ethnic groups. Whilst "suspected child abuse" was a significant factor in the referral of many children, it featured more prominently for Asian children: three quarters of the Asian children had been referred for child protection reasons. "Suspected child sexual abuse" was more likely to be a factor in the referral of white children than black children (16 per cent and six per cent respectively).

- Another noticeable difference was in the identification of mother's mental health as an additional factor in the referral stage. This was cited more often in the case of African-Caribbean and Asian families (31 per cent and 32 per cent respectively) than for children of mixed parentage or white children (19 per cent and eight per cent respectively).

The findings of this study are discussed in the following chapters in the context of qualitative data and the policies and procedures of the selected local authorities. The significance of equal opportunities policies, anti-discriminatory practice, and the Children Act 1989 are brought together to provide a useful framework for discussion.

# Assessment of need and service delivery

## INTRODUCTION

This chapter explores social work intervention with families and children as determined by an "assessment of need". This is a term much used within the realms of social work as it forms a major component of social work policy, practice and provision. Assessment is an evaluation of the most appropriate plan of action for a child and family. It is based on observation, information gathering and appraisal and is followed by professional decision making and action. Assessments are recorded and can form the basis for individual care plans and/or referrals to other services.

The families and children in this study were also subject to needs assessments as defined by their social workers. Because of its primary significance in determining service delivery, our findings and discussion are presented within this framework of needs assessment. The first section focuses on preventative work with families and children; the second addresses child protection; and the third explores the stages of being looked after.

## PREVENTATIVE WORK

Child care studies have repeatedly documented the typical characteristics of families and children who come to the attention of the social services. Most of these families are one-parent, live in local authority accommodation (often poor and inadequate), and are in the low income bracket due to unemployment, insufficient state benefits, or low paid jobs (Packman et al, 1986; Hardiker et al, 1991; Barn, 1990 and 1993).

Whilst poverty, unemployment and disadvantage are pervading influences, this study shows that additional factors such as child abuse and neglect, family relationships, domestic violence, parental mental health, and alcohol and drug problems complicate the equation. Such a multiplicity of factors also point to the particular needs and concerns of families, many of which can only be met following a redressing of various structural inequalities.

Much of social policy and provision in Britain since the advent of the welfare state have been concerned with the addressing of "need". However, the rhetoric about a needs-led approach has never been more forceful than in today's climate of efficiency, "value for money" and quality control. The 1989 Children Act, too, places emphasis upon the provision of services for children considered to be "in need".

## The Children Act 1989

For the purposes of this part (of the Act) a child shall be taken to be in need if,

(a)     he is unlikely to achieve or maintain, or to have the opportunity of achieving or maintaining, a reasonable standard of health or development without the provision for him of services by a local authority under this Part;

(b)     his health or development is likely to be significantly impaired, or further impaired, without the provision for him of such services;
or

(c)     he is disabled.

(*The Children Act 1989*, Section 17(10) and (11), The Department of Health)

"Development" refers to physical, intellectual, emotional, social or behavioural development; "health" refers to physical or mental health.

Local authorities attempt to provide support services to families and children under Section 17 of the Children Act. The nature and extent of such support may differ widely, but operates within the legislative framework outlined above. However, budgetary constraints and limited resources result in  local authorities being encouraged to develop their own interpretations of "need" and strategies to attempt to meet such need. Baldwin and Harrison (1994) argued that definitions of need:

> '. . . *may reflect resource limitations, and therefore carry the risk of being stigmatising and discriminatory. A parent desperately in need of the relief offered by a nursery place may find this difficult to accept if priority is given to children deemed to be at risk.'*
>
> (Baldwin and Harrison, 1994:110)

### Priorities

Preventative work includes work that a social worker can carry out with a family to enable that family to function well and give appropriate care to their child/ren. Preventative work can be useful in helping a family stay together and work through potential conflict situations and prevent them escalating.

This study shows that preventative work was not a priority in the allocation of case work. Priority was given to child protection work in which social workers responded to crisis situations (see Chapter 3). The figure below depicts the level of priority given to cases for allocation purposes, which is essentially governed by statutory duties but can also be determined by limited resources – a situation of potential conflict.

Practitioners and managers participating in this study recognised the importance of preventative work; however, it was stated that it was clearly not viable in the current financial climate:

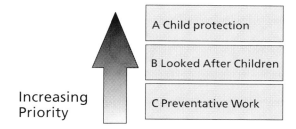

'A great deal of child protection work is carried out by the team here and we have consequently "lost" a great deal of preventative work. I think that in most teams preventative work is perceived as a luxury.'

(Black social worker, Borough)

'Families come to us and say they have a crisis and their child of 11, 12 or 15 has a lot of problems and they need some help. The reaction is well, in terms of our current priorities, your child is "low priority" and we can't allocate him or her. We can only allocate kids who are either on the Child Protection Register, in care, or with disabilities.'

(White social worker, Borough)

The crisis nature of the situation that many families presented to the social services departments in this study meant that there was no time, energy or resources to undertake preventative work. Cases were allocated on the basis of urgency as defined by the social services:

'The fact that some locality teams are understaffed means that a lot of their resources are spent doing "duty" and "stand by" child protection work so they haven't got a hope in hell of getting on with the preventative work. I think they can try and liaise with other agencies and they might do that to support families. They can use Section 17 budgets, most of which are spent. But in terms of resources I think quite simply that we haven't got enough social workers to really put any meaningful preventative packages together.'

(White Area Manager, Metro)

'It is hard to find the time to do that kind of work any more (preventative work) and the result is that you will have contact with the family and will have to do some sort of work with them when a crisis hits; a lot of the work is just crisis work really, like responding to child protection referrals. Also time consuming are the looked after children who aren't in stable placements and are going through placements at a rate of knots and are absconding and in general difficulty. You know, highly disturbed kids.'

(Black Area Manager, Borough)

**Resources**

Lack of sufficient resources was seen as the major problem with repercussions for social work assessment and intervention. In Metro, it was felt that locality teams were particularly under-resourced. Although the department operated a prioritisation system which stipulated that their first priority should be in child protection work, there were shortcomings even in this area.

> 'We have a prioritisation system which tells us that our first priority is investigative work in child protection and we are supposed to allocate all children on the Child Protection Register. We are not even managing to get to that at the moment. In one team, I know that there are at least five children who are registered but haven't got a key worker.'
>
> (White Senior Manager, Metro)

It was felt that this situation had occurred as a result of structural reorganisation in the department, one which did not result in suitable strategies being put in place for long-term effectiveness:

> 'We allowed social workers to opt where they wanted to go to so there was no matching of need, skills or any such criteria. There were just imbalances that we have never overcome. We set up a system that said if Team A had unallocated child protection cases they had to negotiate with the other teams in the Department to get that work allocated, and if they couldn't reach an agreement they came to see the Divisional Managers and we would direct the allocation. They haven't done that and only this week we have reminded them that this is what we expect. But certainly we have teams in this department where they have unallocated child protection cases.'
>
> (White Senior Manager, Metro)

Thus, in Metro, some locality teams had a surplus of senior practitioners while others primarily consisted of inexperienced staff and/or vacant posts.

Metro had also witnessed an increase in child protection work:

> 'We seem to be doing more child protection investigations. I don't know whether that is because we are being more careful about them or whether there is an increase in demand – I really don't know how to explain it.'
>
> (White Area Manager, Metro)

Although the workers and managers in this study emphasised their greater involvement in child protection work rather than preventative work, preventative work is a broad category which should encompass the overall help and support being given to the family. It is not merely a stage at which practitioners engage with families to prevent children from being looked after by the local authority.

For such preventative work to take place, it is essential that social work practitioners possess the skills and knowledge base necessary to work effectively with families. For example, rapport building or establishing and sustaining a good working relationship is a crucial social work skill in early intervention.

Several parents we spoke to felt that they were not being listened to by social services:

> '*All I'm getting is that I'm a bad mother and I don't care about him and that's not true.*'
>
> (African-Caribbean mother)

> '*You can talk till you're blue in the face but at the end of the day they've got the upper hand.*'
>
> (White mother of mixed-parentage child)

## Assessment

There was a feeling of alienation and isolation from the process of assessment by several black and white parents interviewed. There was also a feeling of frustration on the part of social workers when parents they tried to work with were not forthcoming in co-operating with them.

The changing and often constrained role of the social worker was acknowledged by practitioners and managers themselves. Although administrative skills were valued, it was argued very forcefully that basic communication skills were vital in engaging the family to undertake assessments:

> '*I strongly maintain that you need therapeutic skills because when you are working with families and talking them through issues, you need the skills and competencies to be able to do a good assessment and know exactly the nature of the problem you are dealing with, how to link that with available resources and how to encourage families to access these. They (social workers) have to know what resources are appropriate to access and that will only come from a good assessment. So even though we are commissioning services, I do not under-estimate the professional competencies needed in that area.*'
>
> (White Area Manager, Metro)

Preventative work is an area of crucial importance. Families and children in crisis need to be supported to avoid an escalation of problems. Work with minority ethnic families is particularly under-developed in this area (Barn, 1993). Issues of "race", culture, religion and language need to inform the basic framework within which assessments are made and needs are identified and met by using appropriate interventions. These areas are further discussed in this and the following chapters.

| | |
|---|---|
| Metro | 17 |
| All Metropolitan | 38 |
| County | 28 |
| Shire Group B | 33 |
| Borough | 46 |
| Inner London | 64 |
| England | 32 |

**Table 5.1**

**Children on the Child Protection Register: March 1994 (n per 1,000)**
*Source: Department of Health*

## CHILD PROTECTION

National statistics on children who are placed on Child Protection Registers are published annually by the Department of Health. In 1994, when this study was conducted, the proportion of all children in England who were placed on Registers was 32 per 1,000. However, there is great variation across local authorities in the rate of child protection registrations, ranging from a high of 99 per thousand in Lambeth to a low of 11 per thousand in Hertfordshire. (For a more detailed discussion see Gibbons, Conroy and Bell, 1995.) Some of this variation was apparent in the three authorities studied. In all three, the rate of registration was substantially lower than the average for comparable authorities.

Our findings illustrate that child protection work featured significantly in social services area teams; all three local authorities in this study placed child protection at the top of their priority list. This is not surprising considering the statutory responsibility for agencies to protect children from abuse and neglect. In an atmosphere where social work professionals are publicly pilloried for poor decision-making, child protection becomes a highly pressurised area of activity and social workers attempt to follow policies and procedures in a careful manner.

**Figure 5.1**

**Ethnicity of children currently on the Child Protection Register (%)**

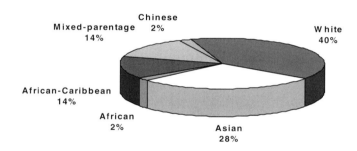

Almost a quarter of the children in our sample (50) were found to be currently on the Register for reasons such as physical abuse (67 per cent), neglect (18 per cent), and sexual abuse (15 per cent). Asian children featured highly in this group and constituted almost a third of the 50 children in this group (28 per cent). Overall, three-quarters of the 28 Asian children in the total sample were, or had been, on the Register.

### Local authority variations

Regional variations between authorities in the rate of registrations were noted. For example, County had the highest number of child protection cases; indeed, County had almost twice the number found in Metro. The majority of children found to be on the Register in County were black children, namely Asian, and those of mixed parentage. Asian children also constituted a significant group in the borough of Metro.

| Ethnic origin | Local authority SSD | | |
|---|---|---|---|
| | Metro | Borough | County |
| African | 0 | 1 | 0 |
| African-Caribbean | 1 | 6 | 0 |
| Asian | 6 | 0 | 8 |
| Mixed-parentage | 1 | 2 | 4 |
| Chinese | 0 | 1 | 0 |
| White | 4 | 7 | 9 |
| Total | 12 | 17 | 21 |

Table 5.2

Local authority variations in Child Protection Register statistics (n)

## Reasons for being placed on the Child Protection Register

We found that the four most frequently used categories for registration were "neglect", "physical injury", "sexual abuse" and "emotional abuse". Almost a third of the sample was found to be on the Register for physical abuse (67 per cent), followed by neglect (18 per cent), and sexual abuse (15 per cent).

Our findings are similar to a recent study which found that black families were over-represented among referrals for physical injury compared to white families, and under-represented among referrals for sexual abuse (Gibbons et al, 1995). Our study shows that "suspected child abuse" was more likely to be a factor in the referral of white children than black children (16 per cent and six per cent respectively, see Chapter 4).

Table 5.3 includes children who had been on the Register on a previous occasion, thereby showing a higher number of 87 (see Total column) compared with a total of 50 (see Table 5.2).

| Ethnic origin | Physical abuse | Neglect | Sexual abuse | Emotional abuse | Other | Total (n) |
|---|---|---|---|---|---|---|
| African-Caribbean | 64 | 27 | 9 | 0 | 0 | (11) |
| Asian | 71 | 10 | 10 | 5 | 4 | (21) |
| Mixed-parentage | 64 | 21 | 10 | 5 | 0 | (14) |
| White | 56 | 15 | 17 | 5 | 7 | (41) |

Table 5.3

Reasons for being placed on the Child Protection Register by ethnic origin (%, Total (n))

We found that black children (Asian, African-Caribbean and mixed parentage) were significantly represented in child protection statistics. Sixty per cent of *all* children on the Register, that is 30 out of 50 in the study sample, were black.

## Child protection and "race"

The high level of black children in child protection statistics presents a rather worrying picture. Interviews with social work practitioners and managers indicated that staff in the three local authorities had an understanding of the conflicts and contradictions this presented within a racial and cultural dimension. In Borough, it was acknowledged that black children were disproportionately represented on the Register. One team had been asked to do a detailed analysis of their cases to see if any causative factors could be identified.

The increased difficulties of working with families when staff did not have an adequate understanding of the cultural backgrounds was acknowledged. For example, in a recent review of a child's death in a Bangladeshi family, a general lack of cultural awareness shown by all the professionals was noted as was poor practice in the use of interpreters:

> 'This review has left us with a dilemma about what to do when we encounter families from a culture that we know absolutely nothing about . . . it is the responsibility of the social worker and Team Manager to actually examine the case and to get the information that would help them to cross the cultural divide.'
>
> (White Senior Manager, Borough)

It is interesting to note that while white managers and practitioners emphasised their lack of cultural knowledge, black workers perceived the same problem from a different perspective. Some felt that Eurocentric child protection procedures were applied universally; they argued that "race" and ethnicity were not adequately taken into account, and this resulted in a discriminatory service to black families:

> 'I have been in situations where people are totally blinded by procedures and they look at each case and say this is a child protection issue and won't make allowances for any cultural factors that may exist.'
>
> (Black Area Manager, Borough)

In interviews with practitioners and managers, we found that child rearing, punishment, and discipline were areas of contention. One white area manager commented that:

> 'Sometimes, some Asian families and African-Caribbean families think punishment is legitimate and if there has been a bit of excess injury, well, it is just one of those things . . . We say well, it isn't really, we can't condone that kind of chastisement in this community.'
>
> (White Area Manager, Metro)

A black manager commented that it was difficult to shake off social workers' attitudes:

> 'If the child has been hit, as far as they (social workers) are concerned, the child has been hit and they are not going to listen to any "excuses" on the basis of "race" or culture and will

*continue with the procedures. You cannot write off those attitudes.'*

(Black Area Manager, Metro)

Metro managers and workers asserted that cultural sensitivity was built into their child protection procedures. Putting this into practice, however, was a wholly different matter.

Other agencies also play a significant role in cases of child protection – the police, health service and schools are often involved from the outset. Their understanding and concerns carry considerable weight. The police are at times involved in removing children from their homes; this is usually done in conjunction with social work professionals. When two statutory agencies come together with a common understanding of the underlying concerns, a smooth operation of their statutory duty should be carried out with sensitivity. It appears that this is far from the actual reality experienced by some black families.

The grounds for removal have been questionable at times and black parents have been labelled as aggressive, unco-operative and violent (Barn, 1993). In this study, a practitioner commented that an emergency protection order (EPO) taken out to remove two black children from their parental home following suspicions of child sexual abuse regarding an older sibling in care, had been, in retrospect, an over-reaction on the part of his agency:

*'Having read the file, I was rather surprised that the EPO was taken. I think, in hindsight, maybe the EPO was unneccessary. It must have been extremely upsetting for the children as well as the mother.'*

(White social worker, Borough)

The two children in this family were removed in the early hours of morning by four white men – two police officers and two social workers. The mother (single parent) was handcuffed and taken in the police van for questioning. This may be an extreme example, but it begs the question of how these situations are allowed to happen. Several months after the incident, the mother was still traumatised by the events. One can only begin to imagine the effect upon her two young children. The children were returned to the family after the court hearing.

One of the initiatives of the Black Resources Team in County was monitoring of the independent chairing of child protection case conferences. Interestingly this had been initiated at the Team's request. This promoted very positive discussions, for example, when was it appropriate and acceptable not to discuss cultural matters for a black child. In the words of the Black Resources Team Manager in Metro:

*'There were some conferences where nothing was explicitly said and yet the assessment was appropriate and the decision was entirely appropriate as well.'*

It is important to note that in several of these cases, most of the workers shared the family's racial and cultural heritage, that is, the practitioners were part of the same community or from a community close enough to give them a comprehensive understanding of the culture of the family. There were implicit shared understandings about the importance and relevance of specific cultural assumptions in specific situations, for example, sexuality in black families or the role of daughters in Muslim families.

Black workers and managers stressed the need to incorporate racial and cultural dimensions into their practice in a sensitive fashion:

> 'What we can't do is go to a black family and say that there are so many cultural issues to address, and so, never mind the child. The child's welfare is paramount and we need to protect that child, and to do so sensitively, taking culture and race into consideration. We have to follow the procedure as laid down for everyone, but there are extra considerations . . . Of course, we still have to do what we have to do but the whole approach has to be managed differently.'
>
> (Black Area Manager, County)

There are a lot of grey areas in child protection work. One of the major difficulties lies in the perceptions of what constitutes "significant harm", and the nature and degree of this in a cultural context. An unquestioning adherence to cultural explanations is not conducive to effective practice. As Dutt argues, whilst an understanding and appreciation of culture is necessary, an obsession with cultural rationalisations is dangerous, and constitutes a gross injustice to black families and children (Dutt, 1994).

## Assessments

Our interviews with both black and white parents showed their lack of involvement in the process of initial assessment. Although parents are increasingly "involved" in child protection conferences, most find it difficult to challenge professional authority. Moreover, parental involvement can, at times, mean nothing more than attending the case conference and being amongst a group of professionals questioning their ability to parent. Thus parental attendance and parental participation are two different matters. Parental participation is a skilful task and requires much planning on the part of both the practitioner and the parent; it has long-term benefits in that it has been shown to be associated with greater success in achieving subsequent family participation (Cleaver and Freeman, 1993).

Communication is vital in keeping everyone informed about the situation. Where English is not the first language of the parent, there are additional factors to consider. We found that interpreters were frequently used in working with Asian families in County. Using interpreters requires great skill and understanding, and it is important that practitioners develop this competency (Baker et al, 1991).

# LOOKED AFTER CHILDREN

Data on numbers of looked after children are published by the Department of Health (DoH) from information provided annually by each local authority. This provides the most accurate source of comparative data over time and between local authorities. At the time this research was being conducted, the latest published data, up to 31 March 1993, contained some gaps where an authority did not submit a return, or a sufficiently accurate return, for inclusion in the national statistics. Unfortunately, Borough was one of those authorities, reinforcing the acknowledged limitations in their management information systems. Table 5.4 below compares the numbers and rate of children looked after in each of the three authorities, and has been drawn from a combination of DoH statistics and those collated locally.

|  | Number | Rate per 1000 |
|---|---|---|
| England | 51,000 | 4.7 |
| Metro | 375 | 5.4 |
| All met districts | 14,100 | 5.4 |
| County | 626 | 3.0 |
| Shire group B | 6,800 | 3.9 |
| Borough* | 443 | 8.7 |
| Inner London | 4,700 | 9.5 |

Table 5.4

**Number and rate of looked after children: March 1993**
* Figures relate to April 1994
Source: Department of Health

## The ethnic origin of looked after children

Although we can present a reasonably accurate comparison of the total numbers of children in public care in our three authorities and contrast this with national statistics, we can not do so in relation to ethnicity. There are no national data on the ethnic composition of children looked after by local authorities; even the revised data schedules introduced after the Children Act do not allow for recording of ethnic or racial origin. Rowe et al (1989) noted that 'the current lack of information about black children in care is serious and startling'. We can only agree and say it is even more serious and startling in 1997.

This issue is discussed more fully in the final chapter. Here we only present data that are available from local databases, which not only help to fill the gaps in national statistics but are also important in relating the characteristics of the population of children in the care system to those of the community. Given the diversity in the patterns of ethnicity within the research authorities, perhaps it is only meaningful to talk about over/under-representation of ethnic groups in the care system in relation to their own locality.

### Metro

The Children's Services Plan for Metro indicated that during the six-month period from January to June 1994, 202 children were placed in foster care.

Of these, 56 were recorded as being from minority ethnic groups. When these figures are adjusted to remove distortions caused by episodes of respite care, this suggests that children from minority ethnic groups represented 20 per cent of all foster placements. During the same period, 28 per cent of placements in residential care were of children from minority ethnic groups. The Children's Services Plan noted that:

> 'Overall, the percentage of non-white children in care is in proportion to population trends and although higher for residential care, the figures available do not lend themselves to make any definite assumptions concerning black children being over-represented in local authority care.'

Unfortunately we were unable to gather any more detailed information from Metro that would enable some analytical breakdown of these figures for children from minority ethnic groups. The largest minority groups of under 18s in Metro were of Indian and Pakistani origin. It would be very useful to be able to relate this information to the ethnic composition of the looked after population.

### County

An effective child care database in County meant that it had information on the ethnic origin of children who received a wide range of social services. These are published regularly in biannual reports. In addition, two special reports had been published: the first, *Black Children in Care*, was published at the end of 1990; three years later, an Audit was conducted by the Black Resources Team, the results of which were published. Both these provided detailed breakdowns of the ethnicity of looked after children. However, lack of consistency in the definitions of ethnic origin between the 1991 Census data and the department's own ethnic monitoring makes direct comparisons of the ethnicity of looked after children difficult. A rough comparison indicates that while children of Asian origin were under-represented, those of African and African-Caribbean origin were over-represented. With respect to children of mixed parentage, if we take the "black other" category as indicating children of mixed parentage, then it would appear that children from this particular background were over-represented in the looked after population.

The ethnic composition for looked after children throughout County are shown in Table 5.5.

### Borough

Unfortunately there were no published or readily accessible statistics on the ethnicity of children looked after by Borough.

### The research sample

Over two-thirds of the sample were looked after children. Of these, 55 per cent were from a minority ethnic background. There were three predominant minority groups in the looked after children statistics, namely

| Ethnic Origin | Number | Percentage (%) | Child pop (%) |
|---|---|---|---|
| African/African Caribbean | 10 | 1.5 | 0.7 |
| Asian | 31 | 4.6 | 13.7 |
| White British/Irish | 579 | 85.8 | 83.3 |
| Mixed parentage | 50 | 7.4 | 0.7 |
| Other | 5 | 0.7 | 1.3 |

**Table 5.5**

**Ethnic origin of looked after children (%): County, June 1993**

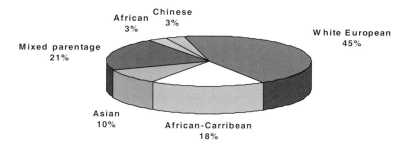

**Figure 5.2**

**Looked after children by ethnic origin (%)**

African-Caribbean, mixed parentage and Asian. Small numbers of African and Chinese children were also looked after.

There has been much concern about the large proportion of minority ethnic children in the care system as previously noted (Barn, 1993). This study focuses on the identification of factors affecting black families and children. The following sections, therefore, address some of the aspects associated with the care process.

## Legal status

Figure 5.3 shows that a significant number of the children in the sample were accommodated under Section 20 of the 1989 Children Act (45 per cent), that is, many of these children had entered care with their parents' consent. In some cases, the child had requested to be accommodated. About a quarter of the looked after sample was subject to compulsory care orders (COs), the remainder were in the early stages of the care process and subject to emergency protection orders (EPOs), police protection (PP) and interim care orders (ICOs). The category of "other" refers to interim supervision orders, supervision orders, privately placed, criminal supervision orders (Sec. 65 Criminal Justice Act), and freed for adoption.

## Reasons for being looked after

Greater numbers of African-Caribbean and mixed parentage children were accommodated with parental or the child's consent than white and Asian children (see Table 5.7). This is interesting given the fact that many of the African-Caribbean and mixed-parentage referrals were about parental

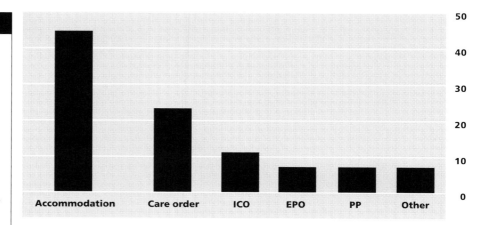

**Figure 5.3**

**Legal status of looked after children (%)**

neglect and suspected child abuse; a significant number of the African-Caribbean referrals were also around concerns about the mother's mental health. There may have been insufficient grounds to prove "significant harm" in the courts, and voluntary agreements were reached with the parents (and in some cases adolescents) to accommodate children.

The reasons for being looked after varied between different ethnic groups. While "suspected child abuse" was a significant factor for many children, it

| Legal Status | African-Caribbean | Asian | Mixed parentage | White |
|---|---|---|---|---|
| Accomm. | 48 | 33 | 48 | 42 |
| CO | 29 | 0 | 22 | 30 |
| ICO | 5 | 25 | 6 | 12 |
| EPO | 5 | 17 | 8 | 7 |
| PP | 5 | 17 | 4 | 4 |
| Other | 8 | 8 | 12 | 5 |
| Total | 100 | 100 | 100 | 100 |

**Table 5.6**

**Legal status by ethnic origin (%)**

featured more prominently in the situation of the 12 Asian looked after children in the sample. For seven of these 12, "suspected child abuse" and the "mother's mental health" were significant factors.

Although the number of Chinese children was small (four), it was noted that the majority of them were also looked after for child protection reasons. All four Chinese children were accommodated. For almost two-thirds of Asian children court proceedings in the form of interim care orders, emergency protection orders and police protection orders were underway.

For African-Caribbean children, "suspected child abuse", "parental neglect", and "mother's mental health" were contributory factors. Mixed parentage children were looked after for reasons such as "suspected child abuse", "parental neglect", "beyond parental control", and "delinquency". "Mother's mental health" was a factor, but less significant than in the case of African-Caribbean and Asian children.

There were four looked after African children: two were accommodated, one was on a care order, and one was on an interim care order.

With the exception of "suspected child sexual abuse", the reasons for being looked after for white and mixed-parentage children were similar in nature. We found that "suspected child sexual abuse" was more likely to be a factor for the entry into care of white children than black children (19 per cent and nine per cent respectively).

## Speed of entry into the care system

It is notable that almost two-thirds of the children became looked after within two weeks of being referred to the social services department (57 per cent). This indicates the "crisis intervention" nature of much of social services work with families and children. Greater proportions of African-Caribbean children became "looked after" within two weeks than any other ethnic group (68 per cent compared with 59 per cent of mixed parentage, 50 per cent of Asian, and 49 per cent of white, see Fig. 5.4).

## Local authority variations

We found that in County and Borough, black children were much more likely to enter care than white children in the first two weeks of referral. In County, it was the Asian and mixed parentage children who entered care more quickly. In Borough, it was primarily African-Caribbean children although smaller numbers of African, Chinese and mixed parentage children also entered care in those early days.

Similar numbers of black and white children were found to be entering the care system in Metro, which had the highest number of admissions in the first two weeks (43 per cent compared with 31 per cent in Borough and 26 per cent in County).

Rapid entry into care is a matter of great concern and raises important questions about the level of preventative work that could be carried out to support black families in need. This could help to obviate the need for children to come into local authority care in the first instance.

## Length of stay in care

### Ethnic variations

African-Caribbean children had been in the care system longer than other groups; 36 per cent of the African-Caribbean children had been in public care for more than five years compared with 24 per cent of children of mixed parentage, 10 per cent of white origin and eight per cent of Asian origin.

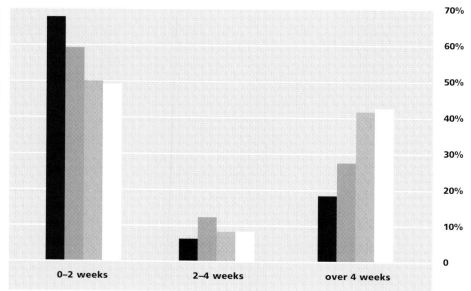

**African-Caribbean** ▮

**Mixed parentage** ▨

**Asian** ▨

**White** ▢

**Figure 5.4**

**Period of time between referral and being looked after by ethnic group (%)**

## Local authority variations

In Metro, about a fifth of the children (19 per cent) had been in care for more than five years; of these the vast majority were African-Caribbean (43 per cent) and of mixed parentage (43 per cent). White children were under-represented in this group (14 per cent).

In Borough, African-Caribbean children were again over-represented as the long-stayers. Of those who had been in care for more than five years, 71 per cent were African-Caribbean and 29 per cent were white.

In County, the situation was different: the two major ethnic groups which featured as long-stayers were those of mixed-parentage and Asian origin (43 per cent and 14 per cent respectively). White children constituted 43 per cent of this group.

## Social work practice

Equality of opportunity – in terms of providing equal access to services and information – and working in partnership with families are the cornerstones of good social work practice. We found that while practitioners and managers spoke in terms of equal opportunities and working in partnership, this was not always translated into practice. A recurring theme during the interviews with social workers and parents was the relationship between the two sides and how this left parents feeling about social services intervention. It would seem that the importance given to Section 22 (5)(c) whilst child protection procedures were underway, diminished. The criteria that informed decision-making were sometimes questioned by practitioners themselves.

> '*Culturally I come from a different background and perspective, and although I'm always aware of the child being at risk, it's important to stand back and weigh up the decision.*'
>
> (White social worker)

The worker was referring to a decision made to accommodate a young man on the grounds of physical abuse; the latter's ethnicity had brought an added dimension to the decision making process.

It is important to question the influences and evidence in decision-making. One black parent recalled how her two daughters were removed from her home early one morning by four white men – two social workers and two police officers.

> *'No females, they were all male . . . the kids were frightened and they asked the social worker, is my mum dead? They handcuffed me in the van and then took my kids away. I don't feel safe, I just can't wait for this supervision order to come off my head, I feel like I'm being watched.'*

(Black parent)

"Insensitivity" and/or "overreaction" based on racial and cultural stereotypes is clearly a factor in the above case. The fact that the children were later returned to the mother calls into question the process of assessment. This particular case highlights some worrying issues which are reiterated in other interviews conducted with parents. One of the key principles underpinning the Children Act is partnership with parents. In order to ensure this, systems should be put into place to enable effective communication and consultation with parents. However, this was not the case for some of the parents we interviewed.

> *'I never knew anything about the Children Act, nobody has ever explained this to me.'*

(White parent)

> *'After the girls were taken away, social services told me they were not able to discuss anything about my daughters with me.'*

(Black parent)

While the safety of the young person should be the primary consideration, the parent also needs to be kept informed of the progress of the investigation. It is important to ensure that parents do not feel as if they are being tried, and once found guilty, have their children taken away from them without being part of the process and understanding it.

For black people, feelings of injustice and prejudice have been first hand experiences within this country. Social services exist to protect children and young people from abuse and neglect and to offer help and support to families deemed to be in need. If social services continue to be seen as heavy handed autocrats perpetuating the injustices of the legal system, then black communities will become even more suspicious of them and partnership will become stifled by lack of trust and animosity, which will benefit neither.

> *'Social services treated me like dirt. They said I was no longer a*

*parent and if I wanted a social worker I should go to the
department where they deal with single people.'*

(Black parent)

Other black parents interviewed had experienced similar feelings of
exclusion:

*'They were treating me as if I was nobody and I had no say . . .
whatever they say goes.'*

(Black parent)

*'Social services don't help, they just want to tell us what to do.'*

(Black parent)

A white parent with a mixed parentage child summed up her feelings when
her child was placed in foster care and entered on the Child Protection
Register.

*'What happened is I became a criminal; it was a police matter. As
far as they were concerned, I had beaten him up and he was now
in care and safe . . . It was really insulting.*

*'They make you feel like an outsider once they've got their hands
on your kid.'*

This parent felt that no assessment of her needs had been conducted, and
that social services had preconceived ideas about her and her situation.

The spirit of participation is not reflected in the experiences of these
parents. Anti-discriminatory work practices which also seek to build
partnerships cannot be left arbitrarily to the goodwill of individual
workers. They must be enshrined in the social work practice and
philosophy of the individual worker, the area teams, the regional
management structure, and ingrained within the strategies of the senior
managers of the social services directorate.

## Care plans

Under the 1989 Children Act, local authorities are required to make adequate
plans for looked after children. It is stipulated that this plan should be in
writing, and that it should be notified to the child and his/her family. The
primary purpose is to help prevent drift in care, and to introduce more
focused strategies for working with families and children.

Although every child being looked after should have a care plan, we found
that this was not the case. Only about two-thirds of the accommodated/
looked after children in the sample (56 per cent) had a care plan.
Moreover, there were enormous regional differences. Whilst almost every
looked after child in Borough had a written care plan (92 per cent), only 41
per cent of the children in County and about a quarter (23 per cent) of
children in Metro had one.

In terms of ethnicity, we found that quite a sizeable proportion of white and African-Caribbean children had a care plan (69 per cent and 64 per cent respectively), whilst only 40 per cent of the mixed parentage and 17 per cent of the Asian children did so. Of the 12 Asian children who were looked after, only two had a written care plan.

Written care plans were not being prepared in a systematic fashion in two of the three local authorities, Metro and County. In Metro, practitioners and some managers perceived them as an administrative nuisance and a burden on their already pressurised time. One senior manager in Metro commented that:

> 'The locality teams are not following procedures in that locality managers are not as stringent about demands for paperwork ahead of the review and the child care plan. An agency worker, who is a very experienced social worker, spent 17 hours filling in review forms for four children for a first review. She was commenting on how the amount of paperwork within the department is onerous – they have to do their own photocopying – because they are not backed up by admin support.'

In one instance, a child had been accommodated for nine months and there was no written care plan anywhere in the department. It appears that the general goals and objectives were understood and professionals 'knew what they were working towards' but it hadn't been written down as per the review requirements.

The vast majority of care plans stipulated 'permanent substitute care' (61 per cent). Permanent substitute care included residential care, long-term foster placements, and adoption. For about a quarter of the looked after children, the plan was to live with their family or relatives.

There were no differences in terms of ethnic groupings except that black children (African-Caribbean, Asian and Chinese) were the only groups of children where placements with relatives and friends were considered. Return to own birth family was not a part of the plan for any of the Asian or Chinese children.

All three local authorities stipulated that issues of "race" and culture were significant considerations in the formulations of care plans. In County, we found that written care plans were not prepared for every looked after child; only 41 per cent of the children had a care plan. However, interviews with managers revealed that written care plans were accorded much importance. The Black Resources Team had given considerable thought to the importance of "race" and culture:

> 'Sometimes they are crucial and sometimes peripheral – no one has mapped out the difference between the two. We find many occasions when workers working transculturally – black or white – can provide an excellent service. At other times, cultural issues

*are more deeply interwoven into the case and a lack of
understanding is not acceptable.'*

(Black Resources Team Manager, County)

**Working with other agencies**

Everyone interviewed thought there had been significant progress in this
area – with additional help available where necessary – for instance, through
co-working and the Black Resources Team. All the teams involved in the
research had access to black staff from a range of cultural backgrounds.
There were also links with some community groups (for example, the
Bangladeshi Youth Group) but access to these was unstructured and
incremental. Overall, there was limited evidence of joint working between
departments in the same authority and with voluntary agencies external to
the authority.

> *'We work too much as individuals on individual cases and do not
> operate as a team.'*
>
> (Black social worker, Metro)

Two social workers who talked positively of joint working, and who were
both involved in partnership work with the juvenile justice team, saw the
benefits in joint working as a means to greater resources.

In Borough, there was no pattern of co-working or developing specialist
advice services. Links to community groups were very informal. A health
project for the Vietnamese community was regarded as a very reliable
resource, but a recent report indicated that few of them were getting access
to social services when they needed help:

> *'The people themselves don't feel confident to approach us and I
> think the social workers are not comfortable in dealing with them
> because they are dealing with people they are not able to
> communicate very well with. Although they do have access to
> interpreters, interpreters are very difficult to develop a proper
> relationship with.'*
>
> (White social worker, Borough)

A black social worker in Borough perceived co-working as a means of
developing the skills of white workers working with black clients: working
with a black practitioner who may have a different perception or approach
could encourage a white worker to take different approaches in their
work.

**SUMMARY**

The concepts of "race" and ethnicity play a significant role in social work
policy, practice and provision. Methods of assessment and provision are
governed by policies and procedures which can be value laden and reflect
the power relationships between professionals and service users. In
situations where local authority social services departments are financially

constrained, the allocation of resources has to be carefully justified.

Assessments of black families and children are less comprehensive and fair when social workers overreact to black family situations. This prevents effective communication between family and practitioners, resulting in the setting up of barriers on both sides.

This is borne out by research studies which continue to demonstrate the high numbers of black children in the care system (Rowe et al, 1989; Bebbington and Miles, 1989; Barn, 1993), rapid entry into care, and longer periods in the care system, as found in this study. Some of our major findings are summarised below.

- Against a backdrop of financial constraints, local authorities are fulfilling their statutory duties in undertaking child protection work, but preventative work with families is less well developed.

- Almost a quarter of the children and young people in our sample (50) were found to be currently on the Child Protection Register for reasons such as physical abuse (67 per cent), neglect (18 per cent), and sexual abuse (15 per cent).

- Black families were over-represented among referrals for physical injury compared to white children, and under-represented among referrals for sexual abuse.

- Over two-thirds of the sample were looked after children. Of these, fifty per cent were from a minority ethnic background. There were three predominant minority groups presented in the looked after statistics, namely African-Caribbean, mixed parentage and Asian. Small numbers of African and Chinese children were also looked after.

- Greater numbers of African-Caribbean and mixed parentage children were found to be accommodated with parental or child's consent than white and Asian children.

- For the majority of Asian children (almost two-thirds), court proceedings were underway in the form of interim care orders and emergency protection orders.

- Higher numbers of African-Caribbean children became "looked after" within two weeks than any other ethnic group (68 per cent compared with 59 per cent of mixed-parentage, 50 per cent of Asian, and 49 per cent of white).

- African-Caribbean children had been in care longer than other groups; 36 per cent of the African-Caribbean children had been in care for more than five years, compared with 24 per cent of mixed parentage, 10 per cent of white and eight per cent of Asian children.

- Only about two-thirds of the accommodated/looked after children (56 per

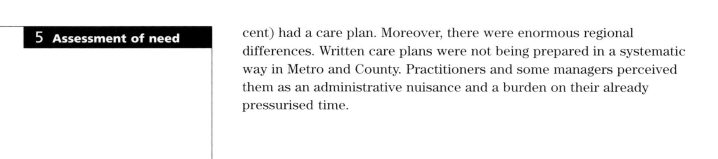

cent) had a care plan. Moreover, there were enormous regional differences. Written care plans were not being prepared in a systematic way in Metro and County. Practitioners and some managers perceived them as an administrative nuisance and a burden on their already pressurised time.

# Placements – Issues and Concerns

*'It may be taken as a guiding principle of good practice that, other things being equal and in the majority of cases, placement with a family of similar ethnic origin and religion is most likely to meet a child's needs as fully as possible and to safeguard his or her welfare more effectively.'*

(DoH, *The Children Act 1989, Guidance*, Vol 3, 2.40)

## INTRODUCTION

In this chapter we examine the placement of children and young people in the three authorities in the light of this guiding principle. First we draw upon the case file studies to provide quantitative data in relation to placement. We then discuss the implications of this in the light of the additional insights about placement issues gained from interviews with children, parents, carers, and social workers.

## PLACEMENT POLICY

In Chapter 3, we discussed the policy positions of each of the fieldwork authorities in relation to placements. We found active application of policies that were broadly in line with those presented in the Children Act Guidance. Although often unaware of any written policy, most fieldwork staff assumed that their authority operated a specific policy of "same race" placement. Senior staff tended to acknowledge that while "same race" placements were likely to be the best option for most children, placement decisions were best made on the basis of the specific needs of each child. In cases where this resulted in a child being placed with carers who did not share the same ethnicity, there was an expectation that plans would be made to ensure that the child's "racial" and cultural needs would be met in other ways.

Given broad acceptance of this 'guiding principle of good practice', how successful were these authorities in achieving this objective? Before considering data from the study, it is worth noting that there was little evidence that these authorities had instituted the mechanisms necessary to monitor the implementation of their placement policies in a consistent and systematic way. Managers had to rely on ad hoc impressions of the extent to which placements in general were ethnically appropriate. Neither Metro nor Borough had the information systems that would make this possible and in County only limited use was made of data concerning ethnicity.

*'I would suspect that we have probably got some children inappropriately placed . . . one of the problems we have is the complete lack of management information. The team couldn't tell me how many placements they made last month, or how many we have in care today or where they are.'*

(Black Area Manager, Metro)

## PLACEMENT PATTERNS

Local authorities are obliged to provide placement details to the Department of Health on an annual basis. Figure 6.1 shows the placement of looked after children in each of the authorities surveyed and compares this to that for England as a whole.

Foster care was the dominant placement in all the authorities, with the highest proportion (70.7 per cent) in Borough. Borough also had the highest proportion of young people in residential care – in private or voluntary homes – although there was a total lack of residential care facilities provided by the local authority.

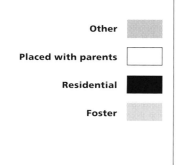

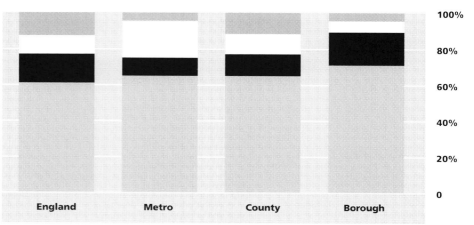

**Figure 6.1**

**Placements of looked after children**
*Source: Department of Health, 1994*

In this study, information was gathered on both the initial placement and the current placement for looked after children in the sample.

### Placement upon entry

The great majority of children from all ethnic groups were placed with foster carers on entry; 75 per cent in all, with 15 per cent going into residential care and 10 per cent to relatives. There were no significant local authority differences in placements, although County used marginally more foster placements.

There were some differences between ethnic groups in initial placements: black children were least likely to be placed in residential care; the proportion of Asian children going into foster homes (50 per cent) was lower than for the other groups, with placements in residential care correspondingly higher. However, this pattern was not sustained in the longer term: almost seven in ten Asian children were placed with foster carers at the time of the research.

### Foster care

At the time of the research, 50 per cent of the children in our sample were placed with foster carers. There were some differences between the authorities in the proportions of the sample who were fostered – 57 per cent in County, 46 per cent in Metro and only 42 per cent in Borough – thus reflecting the success of these authorities in recruiting foster carers. For instance, County had placed a high priority on recruiting foster carers and adopters from minority ethnic groups. Indeed, a video made by County about adoption by Asian parents is on general sale as a training tool. In contrast, Borough had such a shortfall in foster carers overall that a new recruitment campaign had been launched during the research period. Initially, although the publicity material was designed to attract a wide range of people, a more targeted campaign aimed at minority ethnic groups was to follow. One white social worker in this authority described the situation in these terms:

> 'As far as the fostering situation goes, you just have to take what is given, especially with teenagers . . . you just have to have anyone who is available.'

The same worker pointed to the consequences of this when describing the placement history of a white teenager:

> 'The first family was Asian, the second African-Caribbean – with fostering you take what is offered, appropriate or not.'

When a foster service is under pressure in this way, one result is the lack of choice in selecting an appropriate placement. This was clearly demonstrated in an evaluation of the placement outcomes following the decision by Warwickshire to close all their residential homes (Cliffe with Berridge, 1993). The subsequent pressure on that foster care service reduced the possibility of finding a placement appropriate to the child's needs in respect of their ethnic background.

**Recruitment of black foster carers**

All three local authorities had made considerable progress in recruiting foster carers from a wide range of ethnic groups, thereby reflecting the ethnic composition of their looked after children populations (for a comparison with previous research see Barn, 1993; Rowe et al, 1989).

Access to such a diverse group of foster carers increases the capacity of the authority to place children with carers from a similar ethnic group. This was

|  | Metro | Borough | County | Total |
|---|---|---|---|---|
| African | 0.0 | 3.1 | 0.0 | 3.1 |
| African-Caribbean | 31.6 | 40.6 | 10.4 | 26.2 |
| Asian | 13.2 | 0.0 | 31.0 | 14.1 |
| Mixed parentage | 2.6 | 0.0 | 0.0 | 1.0 |
| White | 50.0 | 56.3 | 58.6 | 54.6 |
| Other | 2.6 | 0.0 | 0.0 | 1.0 |
| TOTAL | 100.0 | 100.0 | 100.0 | 100.0 |

Table 6.1

Ethnic origin of foster carers by local authority (%)

clearly indicated in the placements of the children in this sample, as shown in Figure 6.2.

Overall, the majority of children were in "same race" placements, although there was still evidence of children being placed transracially, especially children of mixed parentage. Almost half of the children of mixed parentage were placed with African-Caribbean carers, a small number with Asian carers, and about 40 per cent with white carers. The small number of Chinese children in foster care were placed with white families.

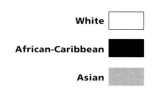

White

African-Caribbean

Asian

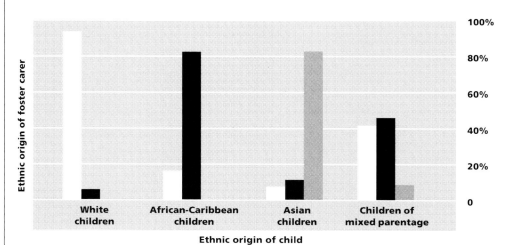

**Figure 6.2**

**Foster care placement by ethnic origin (%)**

**Residential care**

This study found that rather than languishing in residential care, black and white children had a very good chance of being placed in a family setting. Only a small proportion of the children in our sample – 15 per cent – were in residential care. Although Borough no longer had residential provision, it had the highest proportion (17 per cent) of children placed in residential care. Some concern was expressed in all three authorities about the extent to which residential care could meet the cultural needs of children.

Although County operated several residential units, at the time of the research there were few black residents. Management acknowledged that the care offered to children from minority ethnic groups was not of a high standard, a fact noted in a recent inspection by the Social Services Inspectorate (SSI). To address this, an *Equal Opportunities Action Plan for Residential Care* had been devised. A former resident, now living in a private children's home, was clear about why she had requested a move:

> 'They didn't know how to care for black kids; they didn't know about food or hair care or nothing. The other kids were racist but when you told the staff they did nothing about it.'
>
> (Black young woman, County)

Metro had several specialist residential units, but there were also some concerns about them. One young person said he hated it:

> 'They let you go out when you want, do what you want, run away when you want, and don't do anything about it till the police pick you up.'

There was generally a negative feeling about residential care in Metro. Some black residential workers saw this as reflecting on them in a discriminatory way. However, we found evidence of some very good work being conducted by black residential staff in Metro's children's homes, for example, on identity issues.

In Borough, all residential care was in the private and voluntary sector. For some children this meant placements far away from home, sometimes in rural areas. This was particularly difficult for black children especially where the homes had an all white staff group. One young woman who was the only black resident in a therapeutic unit outside the city felt that they could not meet her needs; however, for others the authority had purchased places in a unit which specialised in caring for black young people and this was seen by them as important.

## PLACEMENT ISSUES

The qualitative data on placements suggests four important issues which need to be addressed:

- short-term foster placements;

- meeting the needs of children of mixed parentage;

- meeting the overall needs of minority ethnic children; and

- the complexities of addressing all four factors noted in the Children Act – race, culture, religion and language.

### Short-term foster placements

In discussing placement practice, staff in all three authorities felt able to assert that they would be most unlikely to place a child long term with carers from a different ethnic background; transracial placements were only likely to be agreed in an emergency or on a short-term basis. However, it was clear from the cases in our sample that placements made on such a basis can and do drift into long-term placements. The child is then faced with either more disruption or continuing in a placement that may not meet the needs arising from his or her ethnicity.

> 'I came here just for one night at first; I've been here a year now and don't want to move.'
>
> (Young person of mixed parentage)

> 'I asked for a short-term placement and Michael came when his mother went into hospital. That was two years ago! They are now

*trying to find an adoptive family with a white mother and Asian
father and open adoption . . . If they had known it was going to be
long term, they would have looked for a mixed race family at the
start.'*

(White foster carer)

Finding culturally appropriate placements at short notice requires a foster
care service with considerable capacity and flexibility. However, there are
real dangers in assuming that ethnicity is a less significant issue in the short
term when many of these placements drift into the long term. Authorities
cannot be complacent about this especially if their priorities are based on
false assumptions of what is happening in practice. One experienced foster
carer pointed to the loss of training on caring for children from different
ethnic groups:

*'The policy is that they will try and place black children with
black carers, but they haven't always got the resources. At the
same time they're not training us to care for black children
because it goes against their policies and then sometimes you get
thrown in at the deep end.'*

(White foster carer)

### Children of mixed parentage

Developing policies to meet the needs of children whose parents have
different ethnic backgrounds presents a major challenge. This is no less true
when making placement decisions, especially if there is a divergence of
views between the parent, the child and the professionals. The Children Act
Guidance highlights the issues:

*'. . . choice will be influenced by the child's previous family
experience and . . . by the child's wishes and feelings. In
discussing and exploring these with a child, authorities should
be ready to help the child with any confusion or
misunderstandings about people of different ethnic groups which
may have arisen through previous family or placement
experiences.'*

(DoH, *The Children Act*, Vol 3. para 2.42)

Many of these complexities were raised in the case studies. For instance,
one black mother was very unhappy with the assumptions that had been
made about the needs of two of her children:

*'The baby (mixed parentage) was put with a white family and
the older child (African-Caribbean) with a black family . . .
They're telling me they had no other foster mums. I think they
put her there because she is mixed race, and they thought she'd be
better off with a white family. But they placed my other daughter
with an African-Caribbean family. That was wrong. Why
separate my girls?'*

(Black mother)

This case highlights poor practice and is one in which the needs of siblings, as well as the racial and cultural needs of the mixed parentage child, had not been given due consideration. In the interests of children it is important that, where possible, practitioners work in partnership with parents. This means listening to the parents' views about the kind of placement they wish for their child, taking account of the child's wishes and feelings, and applying professional judgement to ensure that these meet the needs of the child.

In considering the care of children, it is important that practice should help young people 'to develop self confidence and a sense of self worth, so alongside the development of identity and equally important is self-esteem.' (DoH, 1989). A recent research study, although not about the care system, suggests that children of mixed parentage can and do feel very positive about their identity (Tizard and Phoenix, 1993). There is other evidence, however, which suggests that some young people of mixed parentage, especially at adolescence, can display identity confusion and associated low self-esteem (Maximé, 1993; Banks, 1992). This was true of some of the young people in our study and it is important that this is openly discussed and addressed.

The story of Bola demonstrates how some of these complexities were handled in a positive way.

Bola's father was African-Caribbean and he had been brought up by his white mother. A placement with a black foster family did not work out for reasons his mother explained:

> '*He doesn't want to live with black people because he's never lived with black people. He gets on better with white people, he doesn't know the culture of black people.*'
>
> (White mother of mixed parentage child)

After an unsuccessful stay with black carers, Bola was placed in a residential home where he had an experienced African-Caribbean man as his key worker. The worker developed a programme of work which encompassed all Bola's needs, with the added advantage that in him, Bola had access to a positive black male role model.

> '*We started by looking at who Bola thought he was as an individual, with his friends, at home – not just the racial aspect but Bola as a person.*'
>
> (Black residential worker, Metro)

The worker was able to engage with Bola and explore some of his preconceived notions of "blackness"; he built up a picture of his background thereby gaining an understanding of why Bola felt the way he did.

> '*Initially Bola did not see himself as black; black was seen as bad, the people he moved around with were bad and that's what he associated with blackness. All Bola's socialisation had been with*

*white people, all the nice things which had ever happened to him had been done by white people.*

*'Looking at Bola you can't get away from his racial identity. Bola's impressions of blackness were tough, hard, and bad. We spent a lot of time having discussions using books and newspapers as tools for discussion.'*

This placement for Bola addressed most of his needs and challenged some of his stereotyped impressions of black people. This was crucial. As long as Bola held these negative views, his own self-image would be affected, and this was likely to damage his emotional well-being as a black young man.

Similar issues were apparent in the case of Charmaine, another child of mixed parentage. Charmaine also expressed a wish to live with white carers when she was first looked after. However, a placement with black carers who were able to meet her needs meant that she was enabled to develop a positive self image as a black person and was happy to remain with her black carers.

*'When I first went to live with them (black) foster carers, I told them I wanted to live with white people, but now I want to stop here.'*

Charmaine's foster carers described part of their task in caring for her in this way:

*'Charmaine used to identify herself as white. But because she is seen as black (by society) she will experience negativity or racism from white people. So she needs to realise who she is or else it will be a big problem for her in the future.'*

(Black carer)

Foster carer couples in which one was white and one black were a rarity in the three local authorities surveyed. Thus we are not able to give a clear perspective on the success or not of placements of children of mixed parentage with one black and one white carer. One child of mixed parentage in our sample was placed with foster carers in a mixed relationship. The white foster carer, in this situation, highlighted the positive aspects of such placements.

*'Mixed race kids have to expect abuse from both white and black communities – only mixed race couples can understand their experiences.'*

(White foster carer with black husband)

An additional advantage in this situation was the rapport which the foster carer was able to develop with the young person's mother, as white women who had black partners.

*'The foster carer and mother can relate to each other about being*

*in a mixed relationship and the rejection by their white families
because of their black partners.'*

(Social worker)

**Balancing ethnicity with other needs**

Placement decisions are about finding the best available option to meet all
the needs of a child. A holistic framework based on the Children Act and
which addresses the needs of minority ethnic children in a comprehensive
fashion, while taking account of individual emotional and psychological
factors, is essential. The following statement by a practitioner illustrates this
point:

*'They are kids, yes, black kids, but they are still kids. They are
abused and neglected and that happens because they are kids; you
have to start from that point and then take into consideration
their ethnic background.'*

This was highlighted in the case of Harjit, a traumatised young woman of
Punjabi origin who had been brought up as a Sikh. She was received into
care, at her request, following physical and sexual abuse allegations. She
was placed with a Punjabi Sikh family. However, this was the first
experience of fostering for these carers, who had only been approved as
carers the day before Harjit was placed with them. The social worker
highlighted the difficult nature of the placement:

*'The placement happened in an emergency. They (foster carers)
were at a loss as to how to deal with Harjit's feelings around the
abuse, and had to deal with things as they happened. It was
extremely difficult for them as this was their first experience of
fostering. I felt that they would probably not continue with
fostering after this placement.'*

The importance of planning and preparation in a placement is clearly echoed
here together with the need for training and support for foster carers.
Additional resources need to be put in place to address the needs of children
and support foster carers. For instance, in a situation similar to that above, a
worker was able to supplement the efforts of the foster carers by arranging
for therapeutic sessions provided by the NSPCC for the child.

It has to be recognised that attempting to address a range of serious needs
all at once is not easy, least of all for the child concerned. The case study of
Janine, a young woman of mixed parentage, revealed serious concerns about
her self image and her refusal to acknowledge her black parentage. Janine
had also been severely abused. As part of a well formulated care plan, she
was receiving counselling in respect of the abuse she had suffered. She was
also seeing a therapist who specialised in addressing the identity needs of
black young people. In this case the authority had made great efforts to
provide services that would address Janine's needs.

## Race, culture, religion and language

Section 22 (5)(c) of the Children Act stresses the need to address the four factors of race, culture, religion and language. Successful implementation of this Section requires a careful consideration of ethnic diversity and need.

To find placements that exactly match each child's ethnicity is a complex task. It requires a commitment to providing a necessary pool of resources from which to select appropriate carers. This study found that authorities were becoming increasingly aware of these considerations, even if they were not always successful in achieving the objective. Indeed, as one manager reported:

> 'We have had our share of horror stories over the years . . . we had two Asian children placed with Asian carers who couldn't speak their language.'

The complexity of ethnic diversity requires recognition and due consideration. In our study, we found that whilst the vast majority of African-Caribbean and Asian children were placed in families which reflected their ethnic backgrounds, children of mixed parentage were equally likely to be placed in black or white families. Also, in cases where there were only a few children from a small minority ethnic group, their chances of being placed in a racially/culturally appropriate family were minimal. In Borough, for example, Chinese children were placed with white families. This was acknowledged by managers and practitioners in Borough in the context of a general shortage of foster carers.

The lack of appropriate training for foster carers in mismatched placements was also a cause for concern. Borough social services were certainly aware of the problem:

> 'We have a major problem with our foster service. We don't train or support our foster carers adequately. Given that there are likely to be placements that are mismatched either by "race" or otherwise, it is unfortunate that we don't have the systems to compensate for that but we rely very much on the commitment of the foster carers to compensate for that. Sometimes that will be picked up in the planning process and attempts may be made to link the child to community groups or to get an independent visitor, but it is at an ad hoc level. I think this is a major problem.'
>
> (White Senior Manager, Borough)

We found that foster care placements where consideration was given to the child's religious and cultural background were viewed positively. One Asian teenager spoke very admiringly of her Sikh foster carers, and highlighted the benefits of sameness:

> 'It's good because my brothers have got long hair and so have Mrs C's husband and her son – so someone can look after their hair

*here. Also, I get greater understanding.'*

(Sikh young woman, Metro)

Other black youngsters spoke positively about their "same race" placements and welcomed the direct emphasis on their ethnicity by social workers. The benefits of such placements were echoed by a white foster mother caring for a two-year-old Chinese child:

*'A child who is black will feel more comfortable in a black family. But I don't know whether Peter notices or realises he is different. So to me he's just English.'*

(White foster mother)

## POSITIVE STRATEGIES FOR SUPPORTING PLACEMENTS

Matching children with carers of a similar background is likely to be the best option. However, where that is not possible other means must be found to help children develop a positive self-image and take pride in their ethnicity. There were many examples of good practice in using alternative ways to meet racial and cultural needs where these were lacking in a placement.

- An African-Caribbean boy, who was placed in a residential school in Devon with few black staff or companions, was supported in a specialist black residential unit near home during the school vacations.

- A young girl of Chinese origin who had been placed with white carers was befriended by a Cantonese speaking independent visitor.

- A Nigerian boy in private foster care with white carers was befriended by a West African social work student who also worked with him.

- A child of mixed parentage who had problems in acknowledging his ethnic origin underwent detailed identity work with a specialist black therapist.

## SUMMARY

It would appear that the local authorities surveyed were aware of their role and responsibilities under Section 22 (5)(c) of the 1989 Children Act. Our study found that the vast majority of African-Caribbean and Asian children were being placed in substitute families which reflected their own ethnic and cultural backgrounds. Our findings also challenged the assumption that black children languish in residential homes due to non-availability of ethnically matched placements – indeed, when authorities made genuine efforts to attract potential carers from minority ethnic backgrounds, they could be successful. In addition, our case studies provide additional testimony to the establishment of appropriate services and support mechanisms to ensure that the needs and concerns of black children being looked after in residential or foster care were being identified and met.

The placement needs of children of mixed parentage and other minority ethnic backgrounds such as Chinese, were a cause for concern. We found that about 40 per cent of the children of mixed parentage were placed in white families. Due to the non-availability of Chinese families, white families had also been found for Chinese children.

Despite the overall positive picture, there were aspects of placement practice which continued to present real challenges:

- There was an element of complacency about the need to choose carers who were able to meet the ethnic and cultural needs of young people in short-term placements, when experience shows that these often drift into medium or long-term placements.

- Concerns were expressed by staff in each of the authorities about particular aspects of the care provided in residential settings and some of the most negative comments from the sample related to residential care.

- Meeting the particular needs of children of mixed parentage remained problematic; there was a lack of clear policies or practice guidelines on the placement of children of mixed parentage and limited training opportunities for carers in looking after this substantial group of children.

- Planning and preparation of foster placements where the needs of the child were highlighted were needed. Support and training for foster carers also needed urgent consideration.

- While there was a growing undertanding of the need to address "race", culture, religion and language, there were placements in which these had not been fully considered.

# "Race", ethnicity and social work

## INTRODUCTION

This chapter provides an overall framework of the progress and development taking place in the local authorities surveyed with reference to the specific requirements of Section 22(5)(c) of the 1989 Children Act and Section 71 of the 1976 Race Relations Act.

## PRACTICE CONSIDERATIONS OF "RACE" AND ETHNICITY

The underlying theme of the Children Act – that local authorities should attempt to work in partnership with families – is the basis for good practice. Research studies have demonstrated that commonly defined problems and agreed goals lead to more productive and effective outcomes (Wilson, 1985; Olin, 1986). Barn (1993) concluded that 'social workers' ability to conduct appropriate assessments and engage black families to move towards commonly agreed goals will make a marked difference to black child care careers.' (Barn, 1993:122).

This study confirms some of the findings of Barn's 1993 study, namely, that black children enter the public care system more quickly than white children, and are more likely to be accommodated than made subject of statutory care orders. We found this to be the case for African-Caribbean children and children of mixed parentage although Asian children were more likely to be made subject of care proceedings. We were also able to identify elements of good, sensitive practice with black families and children. Although this was based upon case studies and social workers' accounts of their own practice, it does give some insights into practice and service delivery.

### Improved knowledge/skill base

It is heartening to learn that practitioners and managers who participated in this study believed that they were building a useful knowledge and skill base and developing effective methods of intervention. It was notable, however, that social work practitioners' training needs for dealing with "race" and ethnicity were not high on the agenda.

In Borough, there was no longer general training but an individual appraisal system which identified individual training needs; one Area Manager commented that there was commitment to meeting these needs. In County, there had been some debate within the department on the best way forward on "race" awareness training as it had not been offered for four years. Issues around "race" and culture were now included as an integral part of any training, but some felt that a focused training strategy was lacking and that this reflected lack of input by senior management. There was also a view that separate "race" awareness training outside team groups was not necessary nor as appropriate as team development.

## Asian girls and young women

The situation of Asian girls and young women has concerned practitioners for almost two decades (Ahmed, 1981). The needs and problems of this group have been expressed primarily in terms of "culture conflict". Social services departments have not always become involved to offer help and assistance; this has been left to other agencies such as the education and/or the police authorities (BBC, 'East' 1994). Social services have been criticised for inadequate assessments, and for exercising Eurocentric value judgements in their decision-making to the detriment of Asian young women and their families (Ahmed, 1981; Hussain, forthcoming).

### County

This study included seven cases of Asian girls and young women between the ages of 11 and 18 in County. Interviews with staff shed little light on the experiences of these young women and social work practice with them.

Case file information showed that the majority of these girls and young women were referred to social services by the police or the educational authorities. "Child abuse", "parental neglect" and "beyond parental control" had been recorded as significant factors for many of them. This had resulted in accommodation in all but two cases. All of the young women had been placed with foster families on entry into care. Two were now in children's homes, two were placed with Asian foster families, and one had returned to her parents.

Two of the young women, both in their mid-teens, were sisters and had been in care soon after birth because of their parents' drug use. They were of mixed parentage (Asian/white). Their life in care had been far from stable – they had been in six different foster homes and were currently in a children's home.

### Metro

The sample of 61 children from Metro included 10 Asian youngsters. Of these, five were young women between the ages of 10 and 16. "Child abuse" and "beyond parental control" were significant factors for four of these young women. The fifth had been referred by the hospital as a result of her particular disability following a road accident, and was in need of physiotherapy and other help and support. As in County, the other four young women had been referred by the police or the education authorities. Three of the young women had been accommodated – two of them were placed with foster carers and one was placed with grandparents who were currently seeking to be approved as foster carers. Of the two young women placed with foster carers, one was placed with an Asian family, the other with an African-Caribbean family.

With the exception of the two young women of mixed parentage in County, all the others had recently entered public care. In all these cases, there had been complicated family dynamics involving the young woman's relationship with her parents. There were disagreements between professionals and families about the fine line between discipline and child abuse. Social workers became embroiled in very difficult situations. The ultimate resolution was based on the "welfare principle" in which the young person had to be protected at all costs. In coming to these decisions, some practitioners were able to form a good working relationship with the parents in order to achieve their ultimate goal – that of protecting the young woman from further abuse. In other cases, child protection investigations led to marginalisation and alienation of the parents resulting in the child's entry into the care system. There was a noticeable lack of clear strategy in working with the family following entry into care.

Metro practitioners and managers were very positive about their work with Asian girls. In terms of referral, it was felt that Asian girls obviously trusted the police and the educational services enough to seek help from them. Metro staff were working hard to recognise and work with the needs and concerns of both the family and the young woman. The department sometimes acted as a mediator, providing an independent forum for free discussion to resolve difficulties. Workers were aware of myths and stereotypes and the implications of these in hasty decision-making:

*'There are a lot of myths around, especially about Muslim families that they will send the girl back to Pakistan or Bangladesh, or kill her, and so on. I don't think they are that extreme. My feeling has been that I have been surprised at how far parents will go to facilitate the young person because they don't want to lose their young daughter. And very often they love the girl, there is a lot of love in the family, a lot of affection expressed and no matter how traditional they are, I think once they see external authority and some kind of control they have to have trust in the system. I am not sure yet – I can only speak for myself – how much they genuinely trust us. I think the only way they will trust us is if we show them that we understand their community, their social system and their family system . . . I have noticed that the Muslim families we know are opening up more with us than ever before and I think this is because they think we know a bit more than we used to . . .*

*'In fact, some of the girls don't seem in any way deprived. They come in very well dressed, with all the gear, the boots, the denims and all the rest of it. You can see that the parents have gone along, and it is really a process of adjustment. You have got to try and encourage a young person to respect their parents' culture and their parents' attitudes to family and family expectations.'*

(White Area Manager, Metro)

It seems that social work practice for some practitioners and managers has improved considerably. There is a clear recognition of the need to work with both the family and the child and social workers have greater confidence in their own methods of working, and a belief in positive outcomes. In other situations, it would appear that Asian girls would be more appropriately dealt with if they were assessed as children "in need" as opposed to being subjects of formal child protection investigations.

## Use of cultural consultants

Practitioners in this study often engaged black consultants to advise and assist in the assessment on individual cases. Such consultations helped to inform and formulate appropriate care plans and to devise methods by which plans could be implemented.

*'We would make some kind of arrangements for the child's cultural needs to be met by arranging for some significant person in the community to take the child along to, say, a Mosque to meet their religious needs that way. Maybe there could also be opportunities for work with the child to be done by a worker at a family centre.'*

In County, members of the Black Resources Team acted as consultants to white practitioners in assessment and intervention with black families and children.

## Family oriented practice

Interviews with workers and managers revealed that there had been improvements in social work practice with families. It was interesting to note that workers found the family-oriented approach to be more appropriate when working with black families and children, thereby valuing the family as a unit. This method of intervention ensured co-operation and consent in formulating effective strategies.

An experienced white Area Manager in Metro felt that practice with Asian families had improved a great deal in the last decade.

*'Many years ago I would bunch many people together but I am now much more conscious of individuality, like I now understand a lot of issues around Sikhism, Buddhism and Islam and, of course, different strands of Christianity as well, including African-Caribbean and African traditions.'*

Family-oriented approaches, such as systemic family work and family group conferences, were regarded as particularly effective when workers were required to act as mediators between young people and their families. Social workers felt able to provide an environment which facilitated communication and discussion and found compromises to ease difficult situations:

*'We get involved with these families and we are much more aware of the cultural, religious and social dimensions than we were previously and that is not only true for black families but also for white families.'*

Jones and Butt (1995) commenting on an NSPCC project on child protection found that 'NSPCC working conditions, training, supervision and culture of innovation provided opportunities for staff to become highly skilled; yet staff claimed to be unskilled when working with black children and families, and interventions such as therapeutic work, group work and written agreements were rarely offered or developed for black children and families.'

Our findings showed that family group conferences, networking, and family therapy were useful ways of working with black families to bring about positive changes as seen in Metro. Research studies in the United States also point to a higher success rate where such methods are employed in work with black families (Ho, 1987; Paniagua, 1994). Unless and until there is greater family involvement, black children will continue to enter the care system at a rapid rate, and continue to be made subject to child abuse investigations rather than being offered support services.

Sinclair et al (1995) argued that much work with adolescents remained at a superficial level; there was little or no in-depth work undertaken. They concluded that whilst practical help was offered, 'the emotional and psychological needs of the young people often remained untouched and were likely to be carried into adulthood'. In this study, we found limited evidence of in-depth work with black children. Practitioners felt so overwhelmed by the volume of work that therapeutic work with any individual child would be considered a luxury. The sad reality is that while there may be resources to which white children can be directed, the same is not always true for black children.

## ORGANISATIONAL CONSIDERATIONS OF "RACE" AND ETHNICITY

Interviews with managers and practitioners in all three of the local authorities signified that issues around "race" and ethnicity were important considerations when working with families and children. The nature and extent of this recognition differed between authorities. Evidence of specific mechanisms to facilitate discussion around "race" and culture was found to exist primarily in Metro and County. Borough, the London authority, had placed "race" and ethnicity high on their agenda – but that was in the 1980s, and much of that momentum had diminished. The management attitude was one of 'we do this anyway', while some practitioners felt unsupported by lack of formal structures and training.

We found that there were general issues of discontent about administrative requirements resulting from the Children Act 1989. Front line workers belived it had generated more paperwork and bureaucracy. In Metro, for example, implementation of the Act had had to take second place due to departmental reorganisation. As the department reorganised into generic teams, the National Health Service and Community Care Act 1990 became the major preoccupation for 12 months. The Children Act and its implementation had to be put 'on the back burner'. As a consequence of these upheavals, insufficient consideration was given to the recruitment and deployment of staff within childcare services. This undoubtedly had an impact on services to both black and white families.

Lack of resources was another significant general factor and had direct impact on the specific needs and concerns of black families and children. The marginalisation of their needs and concerns meant that in the face of financial cutbacks, resources directed towards black families were the first to disappear as their existence seemed harder to justify by agencies trapped in the confusion of "ethnic sensitivity" and "anti-racism", particularly in the wake of the "political correctness" backlash.

In their attempts to provide a service to black families and children, all three agencies had recruited black staff and made use of interpreters and community development projects. However, this was not as a direct result of Section 22 (5)(c) of the Children Act 1989, although this conferred greater legitimacy on the relevant policies and practices. Indeed, all three agencies had well developed equal opportunities policies and had been grappling with "race" and ethnicity issues and how best to meet the needs and concerns of black children.

In Borough, equal opportunities had been on the agenda since the early 1980s. This had led to the recruitment of black staff and the identification and development of training needs in addressing issues arising from "race" and racism. Issues of "race" and culture had also informed the placement needs of black children. Ten years on, much of the initial vigour and enthusiasm had died down. Now there was little mention of training needs or the importance of "race" and culture in placement practice. Practitioners and managers spoke of awareness of "race" and ethnicity, but highlighted the financial constraints of meeting such needs appropriately.

In Metro, the situation was very similar. "Race" and ethnicity were on the agenda in the 1980s, but were now given less significance:

> 'I think there were a few initiatives years ago, such as employing 16 interpreters in the department, buying in packages for training, the work of the Racial Identity Panel, the work on "same race" placement policies . . . The Adoption Panel has done a lot of work as has the Fostering Panel. You have got quite a good mix in those groups now. But I think we are losing it a bit at the moment.'
>
> (White Senior Manager, Metro)

It would appear that many of the equal opportunities structures had been put in place, and there was still some optimism. For example, in Metro, the Racial Identity Panel had been set up as a result of the negative experiences of children of mixed parentage in white foster homes. The panel existed to identify and assess identity needs of black children and to support workers in identity work.

In Metro, there was also a greater recognition of the role of the practitioner in working with black families to achieve positive outcomes. The development of the worker's own knowledge base and skills was considered to be crucial.

The development of equal opportunities in County was more recent. Practitioners and managers demonstrated greater enthusiasm and optimism. Staff were eager to portray themselves and their locality as pioneering good equal opportunities. As discussed earlier, County had a Black Resources Team which acted as consultants to managers and practitioners. It had also carried out its own research on local area teams to examine service provision to black families and children. The team's brief had been extended to do more direct work with children, co-working alongside social workers on issues of "race", culture and identity. It was envisaged that members of the team would be available as an additional resource to help assess and meet the cultural and racial needs of black children. The constraints of such joint working have not been covered in this study but would be an area worthy of exploration in the light of previous work in which black workers have reported feelings of marginalisation and hostility from white colleagues (Stubbs, 1985; Barn, 1993).

## EMPLOYMENT OF BLACK WORKERS

All three local authorities had made efforts to recruit black staff, particularly African-Caribbean and Asian workers. In terms of racial matching of worker and client, a significant proportion of the black children had been allocated a black worker although not always from the same ethnic background. The vast majority of African-Caribbean children had an African-Caribbean worker (78 per cent); almost 50 percent of the Asian children were allocated an Asian worker; all ten of the African children had an Asian or African-Caribbean worker; and over 50 per cent of the mixed-parentage children had an Asian or African-Caribbean worker as did almost all of the Chinese children.

It seems that in all three authorities, consciously or unconsciously, a policy of racial matching of client and worker was in operation. It was clear that a majority of cases involving black children were allocated to black workers. Although we have been able to highlight examples of good practice carried out by black workers because of their particular skills and knowledge base, we are concerned that white workers may not have been given opportunities to develop their practice with black families and children – if their practice remains inconsistent, there is little likelihood of consolidating their skills and understanding.

A policy of racial matching in the allocation of work may be necessary and important in some situations; however, such a policy has to be consciously applied and pro-active, and not the result of muddled thinking. It can lead to the isolation and marginalisation of black workers who may face high expectations that they may not always be able to meet.

'If a complex "Punjabi" case comes along there are subtle pressures placed on me to pick it up.'

(Asian social worker, Metro)

Social work literature is full of references to mutual respect and understanding, and recognises these as crucial prerequisites for effective communication, goal-setting, and intervention. Our study shows that many black practitioners were able to engage with black families and children and work in appropriate ways to bring about mutually agreed goals.

We found that Asian female workers were able to relate effectively to young Asian women who were experiencing difficulties at home.

> 'In my work, I can relate to certain situations and I try to put over that I have been through similar ones myself so that the clients know they are not the only ones and don't feel as isolated.'
>
> (Asian social worker, Metro)

Racial and cultural understanding are prerequisites if practitioners are to gain the trust and confidence of black families. Workers need to begin to operate sensitively to effect change. They need to avoid over-reaction, panic and inappropriate decision-making – all of which have highly detrimental consequences for black families and children.

This study found that minority ethnic clients valued rapport and understanding which led them to have confidence in the worker. Families were able to identify the positive aspects of working with practitioners from a similar ethnic background:

> 'It was a lot easier to deal with people from a Gujarati speaking background . . . especially with the letters. I was able to understand what was expected.'
>
> (Asian mother)

Practitioners demonstrated a complex understanding of family dynamics within a cultural framework:

> 'It is hard to explain to a white person what it's like to be an Asian woman – your parents may be strict, perhaps they don't let you stay out late, you may be expected to have an arranged marriage. . . Some people just don't understand. They think they (the girls) need protecting and take them away, they don't understand the cultural aspects of the situation. They remove them from their home and isolate them completely from their community and family. They need to think what steps they are going to take, perhaps in consultation with others, instead of acting like a bull in a china shop.'
>
> (Asian social worker, Metro)

However, working with Asian families presents its own problems for Asian social workers. Being Asian does not mean automatic entry and immediate rapport. For example, in the case of a teenage Asian girl, the mother perceived the young Asian female worker as a corrupting influence, and not as someone who would be fair-minded and mediate between the child and family.

Once the Asian worker has built up trust and confidence, he/she is able to be effective in their work and more able to work with the family to bring about positive outcomes. For example, in the case of the rebellious teenager mentioned above, the Asian social worker was able to set boundaries with her because of her understanding and awareness of Asian traditions and expectations.

Thoburn et al (1995) documented the effectiveness of black social workers in black family situations:

> 'The family was of Asian origin and because the social worker was Asian she was able to persuade the father's psychiatrist to modify his approach by producing a full family history for him, which stressed the ethnic background and its relevance to their experiences. She was able to empathise with all the family members.'

> (Thoburn et al, 1995:201)

Thoburn et al (1995) also found that where workers failed to involve black families, decisions were made on inadequate information. This often occured as a result of poor level of communication between family and worker where barriers can be erected, consciously or unconsciously, by both parties.

## Addressing needs and concerns

There are historical factors in defining need in the context of the welfare state, its rationing devices, and perceptions about deserving/non-deserving clients. Due to policy neglect of the needs and concerns of black families and children, an ad hoc and incremental approach continues to exist. Policies need to be developed which do not pigeon-hole black family needs as a problematic area in terms of resources. Social workers need to feel confident in making appropriate assessments where needs and concerns are identified clearly with the family and which, more importantly, can be met from mainstream budgets. There is a desperate need to move away from the marginalisation of needs and funds which only serve to signal a message of misunderstanding, distrust, fear and division.

Our interviews with senior managers suggested that in a climate of financial cutbacks, initiatives to develop services for black families and children are the first to disappear.

> 'The biggest threat that we have is the financial constraints. I think it is incredibly difficult to hold onto the important factors in terms of developing services, particularly for disadvantaged groups whether they happen to be disabled people, or black people, or whoever. Being constantly constrained in what you do means your focus becomes narrower and narrower all the time . . .

> 'For instance, we had something called a multicultural training unit, which was a specific part of the training section and we had to cut that section. We had to make savings and it had to go.

*There are other examples where there have been specific initiatives set up which have had to be lost. I know they are needed because sometimes you can't get moving until you have got them but they are very vulnerable. I think it is very important to try to get the whole thing integrated so well into the fabric of our practice that you can't actually take it away. And so it survives in the same way, or at the same level, that other services survive at the very least.'*

(Manager, Metro)

An integrated approach which attempts to meet the needs of both black and white families would be ideal if it could be made to work. In a society in which black people are still perceived as the "alien" within, welfare services find it hard to accommodate the needs of black families and children in an adequate manner.

## SUMMARY

This chapter has shown that consideration was given to the needs and concerns of black families and children in the three local authorities. Although there were some positive developments, there is little reason for complacency. The financial hardships faced by local authorities meant that service provision to black families and children remained patchy and incremental.

- A lack of a clear training strategy in "race", ethnicity and family work was noted in all three local authorities.

- In spite of the haphazard nature of the training available, some practitioners and managers felt that they were building a useful knowledge and skills base and developing effective methods of intervention. Staff in Metro were able to give practice examples from their work with Asian families and young women.

- A family oriented approach, such as systemic family work and family group conferences, was regarded as particularly effective when workers were required to act as mediators between young people and their families.

- Cultural consultants were seen as a useful resource to enhance one's understanding of racial and cultural issues, and to ensure due consideration was given in practice.

- Lack of resources was a significant general factor but one which had direct impact on the specific needs and concerns of black families and children.

- All three local authorities had made efforts to recruit black workers, particularly African-Caribbean and Asian workers. In terms of racial matching of worker and client, we found that a significant proportion of the black children had been allocated a black worker. Black workers demonstrated a particular effectiveness and sensitivity in working with black families.

# Summary and Recommendations

This chapter brings together the major and significant findings of our study, and puts forward recommendations for social services agencies to consider in their work with black families and children.

We begin with a brief reminder of the aims of the study and its context in terms of the characteristics of the social work areas which acted as research sites. Next is a summary of the findings from the quantitative study. This leads to an outline of aspects of policy and practice which were highlighted by the study. The chapter ends with some recommendations for the development of policy, practice and provision in social services work with children and families from different ethnic groups.

## THE AIMS AND METHODS OF THE STUDY

The broad aim of this study was to examine the way in which the requirement of the Children Act 'to give due consideration to the child's religious persuasion, racial origin and cultural and linguistic background' was reflected in practice within social service departments. More specifically the research sought to determine any differences or similarities in the services offered to children and their families from different ethnic groups.

The study has three components:

- a quantitative file study of 196 children whose cases were allocated to social workers working in seven different teams in three local authorities;

- a qualitative enquiry involving in-depth semi-structured interviews with social work practitioners, middle and senior managers, foster carers, and birth families and children;

- an examination of policy and procedures in three local authorities.

## THE RESEARCH SITES

The research was undertaken in three local authorities:

- County, a shire county in the East Midlands;
- Metro, a metropolitan authority in the West Midlands;
- Borough, a London borough.

In part, these authorities were chosen because they served populations with substantial and diverse minority ethnic communities. In addition, the particular social work areas within those authorities in which the research was located were, in the main, the areas with the highest concentrations of black people.

The characteristics of the population of looked after children in these authorities were representative of their authority group as a whole. This suggests that despite the higher than average black population in these areas, the findings from the study will have widespread applicability and the messages from this research will be of relevance to others.

## RESEARCH SAMPLE

The research sample consisted of 61 children from Metro, 71 from Borough, and 64 from County; it included 105 girls and 91 boys. With respect to ethnic background, there were 109 children from minority ethnic backgrounds, and 87 who were white.

The criteria employed for including children in the sample was the allocation of a social worker. This rendered a sample which included not only looked after children but also those on the Child Protection Register and others receiving family support services.

Almost 50 per cent of our sample came from a one-parent family, primarily mother-headed (47 per cent). The remainder were from two-parent families (39 per cent), and extended families (nine per cent) or other types of families (five per cent).

Less than a quarter of the sample was under the age of five (22 per cent); 34 per cent were between the ages of six and 12, and the majority – 44 per cent – were 13 and above.

## DIFFERENCES BETWEEN ETHNIC GROUPS

A quantitative analysis of case file information yielded considerable detail about the referral process, assessment, and provision of services to children and their families, in relation to ethnicity. Some of the major findings are summarised below.

### Referral and assessment

- Asian and African-Caribbean parents were least likely to refer themselves to the social services for help and assistance. It was interesting to note that a significant number of mixed-parentage children had been referred by their parents (mostly white mothers).

- Proportionately more black children than white were found to be subject to child abuse investigations. Almost all the difference was attributable to the high numbers of Asian children on the Child Protection Register.

- The reasons for children entering the care system varied amongst different ethnic groups. While "suspected child abuse" was a significant factor for the referral of many children, it featured more prominently in the situation of the 12 Asian looked after children in our research sample.

- Another noticeable difference was in the identification of mother's mental health as an additional factor in the referral of families to the social services. This was cited more often in the case of African-Caribbean and Asian families (31 per cent and 32 per cent respectively) than for children of mixed parentage or white children (19 per cent and eight per cent respectively).

- With the exception of "suspected child sexual abuse", the reasons for being looked after for white and mixed-parentage children were similar in nature.

- We found that "suspected child sexual abuse" was more likely to be a factor for the referral of white children than black children (16 per cent and six per cent respectively).

## Looked after children

- Although within our sample a higher proportion of black children was looked after than white children, the overall lack of detailed management information precludes any clear conclusions about "representativeness". In County, where some information was available, children of African-Caribbean and mixed parentage were found to be over-represented compared to their proportion in the general child population. Asian children were under-represented.

- As in other studies, this study showed that the two largest groups of black looked after children were African-Caribbean and mixed parentage.

- In terms of legal route of entry into "care", African-Caribbean and mixed parentage children were more likely to be accommodated with parental or young person's consent than white and Asian children.

- For the majority of Asian children (almost two-thirds), court proceedings were underway in the form of interim care orders and emergency protection orders.

- It is significant that almost two-thirds of the children and young people became looked after within two weeks of being referred to the social services department (57 per cent). This indicates the "crisis intervention" nature of much of social services work with families and children.

- Higher proportions of African-Caribbean children became looked after within two weeks than those of any other ethnic group (68 per cent compared with 59 per cent of mixed parentage, 50 per cent of Asian, and 49 per cent of white children). Such rapid referrals into care are a matter of great concern, and raise important questions about the level of support services to families in need to obviate entry into public care.

## Care and care plans

- Although every child being looked after should have a written care plan, we found that this was not the case. Only just over half of the looked after children (56 per cent) had a care plan. Moreover, there were enormous area differences. Whilst almost every looked after child in Borough had a written care plan (92 per cent), only 41 per cent of the children in County had a care plan followed by only about a quarter (23 per cent) of the looked after children in Metro.

- In terms of ethnicity, we found that quite a sizeable proportion of white and African-Caribbean children had a care plan (69 per cent and 64 per cent respectively), while only 40 per cent of the mixed parentage and 17 per cent of the Asian children did so.

- To meet the requirements of Section 22 (5)(c) of the 1989 Children Act, it is important that information is recorded systematically about the child and family's racial, cultural, religious and linguistic background. This study showed that while information about the child's ethnic origin was usually available, other data were difficult to ascertain. Indeed, religious background had only been recorded for 50 per cent of our sample.

- African-Caribbean children had been in care longer than other groups; 36 per cent of the African-Caribbean children had been in care for more than five years, compared with 24 per cent of the children of mixed parentage, 10 per cent of white and eight per cent of Asian children.

## Placement of looked after children

This study found that the vast majority of white, African-Caribbean, and Asian children were placed with families which reflected their own "race" and ethnicity. The situation of mixed parentage children was, however, somewhat different. They were equally likely to be placed with a white or an African-Caribbean family. A small number were placed in Asian families. The four Chinese children were placed transracially with white foster carers. Of the three African children, two were placed in black families (African and African-Caribbean), and one child was placed transracially in a white family.

Our qualitative data suggests that greater recognition of the complexity of ethnic diversity was required in all three of our local authorities.

We found that the number of children being placed within residential homes was small. Both black and white children had a very good chance of being placed within a family setting.

## ASPECTS OF POLICY AND PRACTICE

These quantitative findings, together with data gathered from interviews, raise important issues in relation to policy and practice in service provision to black children.

## Policy development

All authorities had adopted equal opportunity policies in respect of employment and service delivery, although there was less evidence of implementation of anti-discriminatory policies or procedures. Policy in other areas such as placement choice – especially for children of mixed parentage – was very unclear. As a consequence, many staff assumed, indeed quoted, departmental policies which did not exist or were out of line with the position of more senior managers. There were no written policies with respect to the placement needs of minority ethnic children.

## Equal opportunity policies

What was the impact of these equal opportunity policies? In terms of staffing, at team level local authorities had made enormous efforts to recruit a more ethnically balanced staff group which reflected the local population being served. This was less true of middle managers and even less true of senior managers.

The mechanisms for monitoring the ethnic composition of staff, service users and target populations varied from reasonable to very poor. Even where such mechanisms existed there was little evidence that they were used effectively.

The fact that central government has not taken a lead in encouraging ethnic monitoring causes concern.

Training for staff and carers on equal opportunities and anti-racist practice was very sparse and lacked any impetus.

## Placement policies and practice

Despite some lack of clarity in policy, most staff had a good general sense of appropriate criteria to apply in choosing a placement. However, an important exception to this was in relation to children of mixed parentage. This issue requires much more discussion among staff and their managers.

Similarly the ethnic diversity of our population requires policies and practices sophisticated enough to incorporate the totality of a child's needs and concerns. This highlights a training need, but also the need for departments to consider carefully how they can ensure the availability and support of foster carers from a wide range of different backgrounds.

Departments were relatively confident about finding suitable long-term placements and this is borne out by our sample, but they seemed to attach less importance to short-term placements, despite the tendency for short-term placements to drift into long term.

Standards in residential care, especially in implementing anti-racist approaches, were a matter of some concern.

## Assessing and meeting need

In meeting the needs of black children much of the focus is on placement. Yet, as our earlier chapters demonstrate, many other aspects of service provision can enhance or detract from this objective.

Assessment of the needs of children and families requires that staff build a rapport and understanding with their clients. Working in partnership can be more difficult where staff and users have different ethnic backgrounds. Departments must take all necessary steps to ensure an equitable service, for instance, training the staff group adequately to deal with clients from different ethnic groups; developing and supporting an ethos of anti-racist, anti-discriminatory practice; putting in place arrangements to allocate staff of the same ethnicity where appropriate; a good, readily accessible interpretation service; the establishment of internal specialist advisors or the employment of external consultants and advisors; partnerships and links with local communities. While we were encouraged to find some evidence of all these strategies, our research also pointed to deficiencies in all these areas.

## RECOMMENDATIONS

The research evidence from the three local authorities studies suggests that there have been significant improvements in recent years in social service provision for black children and families. Staff in all three local authorities were aware of the importance of providing an ethnically appropriate service and there were examples of notable efforts to achieve that. There was also a clear recognition of the need for further achievement. The need to address issues of "race" and ethnicity, and to develop and strengthen skills, was emphasised by managers and practitioners.

This leads us to suggest a number of recommendations for change. These recommendations, which are grouped under five headings, are aimed at central and local government. Those addressed to local authorities reflect the relevant sections of *Racial Equality Means Quality*, the Commission for Racial Equality's standard for local government (CRE, 1995).

### Ethnic monitoring

Effective monitoring of policies in respect of services to children from minority ethnic groups requires good information systems which record details of the ethnicity of children and families, carers and staff. Moreover, it is important that such information is made available and used proactively to plan, provide and monitor services. Comparative analysis over time and between different areas requires information at a community level for the local authority, and at a national level.

**Central government**: It is recommended that the Department of Health (DoH) takes a lead in ethnic monitoring by requiring all social services departments to supply information on the ethnic origin, religion and language of children in receipt of services. The DoH should amend all statistical returns to include ethnicity, for instance, in respect of children looked after by the local authority and those on the Child Protection Register. Such information should also be included in the annual report published by the DoH, *Staff of Local Authority Social Services Departments*. The DoH should develop, publish and promote new guidance to local authority social services departments on effective practice in ethnic monitoring.

**Local authorities:** It is recommended that all local authority social services departments collect information about the ethnicity of children and families with whom they are in contact, including recording their religion and language, and of carers and staff. This information should be published regularly and made available at every level within the organisation. The implications of such information for planning and provision of services should be regularly considered by managers and practitioners.

### Policy guidance

Managers and practitioners will be greatly assisted in implementing both the spirit and the letter of the Children Act 1989 and the Race Relations Act 1976 by developing clear policies at corporate and Directorate level. These should address equal opportunities in employment and in service provision and inform procedures and practice. Policies need not be dogmatic, rather, they should set standards and establish guidelines that enable staff to make appropriate decisions for individual children. To be effective, policies must be monitored and reviewed. It is vital that all staff are aware of departmental policies.

**Local authorities:** It is recommended that all local authorities establish written policies on equality of opportunity in employment and service delivery. Furthermore, authorities should develop policy guidance on key aspects of social services such as ethnicity and child care placements, and allocation of cases. Policies should incorporate strategies for their implementation and monitoring.

A written copy of the policies should be made widely available to all staff.

**Practitioners:** It is recommended that practitioners should understand and act upon agency policies, guidelines and procedures.

### Training

Appropriate and adequate implementation of the Children Act 1989 and the application of departmental policies require a high level of awareness and skill among staff. This can be advanced by a programme of staff training and development. There is a need for more appropriate training in developing race/cultural awareness and anti-racist and anti-discriminatory practice, and also in developing better and more informed strategies which will increase confidence in staff and enhance policy and practice in working with black families and children. It is essential that appropriate training takes place at all levels within the organisation.

**Central government:** It is recommended that the DoH should commission training material, in the context of the requirements of Children Act 1989, which deals specifically with meeting the needs of minority ethnic children. The production of specific training packages and guidance is required to enable practitioners to develop confidence and skills in working with minority ethnic families and children.

**Local authorities:** It is recommended that local authorities review the training needs of all staff individually in respect of equal opportunities and anti-racist training and develop an effective strategy to meet those needs. The use of individual and group supervision could be effective in highlighting training needs and, to some extent, addressing such need.

Similarly, the training needs of black and white foster carers should be reviewed regularly and met accordingly.

**Practitioners:** It is recommended that practitioners examine their own cultures, values, attitudes, behaviour, and knowledge about black people's lives and incorporate anti-racist training as part of their ongoing professional development.

### Resource provision

Meeting the needs of black children and their families requires appropriate resources. These include:

- a staff group which reflects the ethnic composition of the local community and possesses the necessary skills and attributes to engage and work effectively with black families and children;

- sufficient placement options to offer a choice and match with assessed needs;

- building strong links with local communities;

- easy access to high quality interpretation and translation services.

**Local authorities**: It is recommended that all local authorities review their allocation of resources to meet the needs of black children and families in a systematic way. Where gaps are identified, strenuous efforts should be made to fill these. In particular, it is recommended that local authorities examine the adequacy of resources to allow the following:

- provision of, or access to, sufficient residential placements which can clearly meet the needs of black children;

- recruitment, preparation and training of sufficient foster carers who reflect the racial, cultural, religious and linguistic background of the looked after population to ensure availability of choice of suitable foster placements, both short and long-term;

- access to a range of resources, such as independent visitors or community groups, to support children and young people where their carers are unable to meet all their racial and ethnic needs;

- ready access to excellent translators and interpreters. Agencies need to make greater efforts to find appropriate interpreters who speak the same dialect. It is crucial that interpreters are trained to work sensitively and effectively in casework with individuals and families, as well as more formal settings, such as Child Protection Case Conferences and court proceedings;

- development of strong links with black and minority ethnic communities, establishing trust and building active partnerships in promoting the welfare of children;

- use of specialists/consultants to enhance and complement existing departmental expertise and assist staff where they feel ill-equipped to address the racial and ethnic needs of a child or family.

**Practice issues**

Effective practice requires the appropriate infrastructure – policies, resources, training, information, and monitoring systems. Our recommendations above have addressed these issues.

Arising from the evidence of this study, we make suggestions for improvements to individual practice. It is recommended that:

- staff undertake training to understand the cultures of the many local minority ethnic communities, acquaint themselves with their main community organisations, and keep informed on local news and issues;

- staff develop more sophisticated approaches to ensuring that all aspects of ethnicity are taken into account, and that more considered thought is given to understanding all the needs of minority ethnic children;

- practitioners ensure that they are using appropriate assessments of needs and risks, based on relevant information;

- practitioners develop their skills in working through and with interpreters;

- practitioners employ a range of appropriate social work approaches for working with black children, such as family work, group work, and direct work with children. Recognising that that there may be limitations in traditional approaches that adopt Eurocentric theories and methods, practitioners need to understand and know each child and tailor their work to best meet the needs of that child.

# Bibliography

Ahmad, B. (1990) *Black Perspectives in Social Work*, Venture Press

Ahmed, S. (1981) 'Asian Girls and Culture Conflict' in J. Cheetham et al, (eds) *Social and Community Work in a Multiracial Society*, London: Harper & Row

Ahmed, S. (1981) 'Children in Care. The Racial Dimension in Social Work Assessment' in J. Cheetham et al (eds) *Social and Community Work in a Multiracial Society*, Harper & Row

Ahmed, S; Cheetham, J. and Small, J. (eds) (1986) *Social Work with Black Children and their Families*, British Agencies for Adoption and Fostering (BAAF)/Batsford

Amin, K. with Oppenheim, C. (1992) *Poverty in Black and White: Deprivation and Ethnic Minorities*, Child Poverty Action Group, in association with the Runnymede Trust

Bagley, C. And Young, L. (1982) 'Policy Dilemmas and the Adoption of Black Children', in Cheetham, J. (ed) *Social Work and Ethnicity*, Allen and Unwin

Baker, P; Hussain, Z and Saunders, J. (1991) *Interpreters in Public Services*, Venture Press

Baldwin, N. and Harrison, C. (1994) 'Supporting Children in Need: The Role of the Social Worker', in David, T. (ed), *Working Together for Young Children*, Routledge

Banks, N. (1992) 'Techniques for Direct Identity Work with Black Children', *Adoption and Fostering*, 16(3), 19–25, BAAF

Barn, R. (ed) *Direct Work with Black Children and Young People*, BAAF, forthcoming

Barn, R. 'White Mothers, Mixed-Parentage Children: A Preliminary Discussion', *British Journal of Social Work*, forthcoming

Barn, R. (1990) 'Black Children in Local Authority Care: Admission Patterns', *New Community*, 16(2), pp 229–46

Barn, R. (1993) *Black Children in the Public Care System*, BAAF/Batsford

Barn, R. (1994) 'Race and Ethnicity in Social Work: Some Issues for Anti-Discriminatory Research', in B. Humphries and C. Truman, (eds) *Rethinking Social Research*, Avebury

Batta, I. and Mawby, R. (1981) 'Children in Local Authority Care: A Monitoring of Racial Differences in Bradford', *Policy and Politics*, 9(2), 137–149.

Bebbington, A.C. and Miles, J.B. (1989) *The Background of Children who enter Local Authority Care*, British Journal of Social Work, 19 (5)

Beresford, P; Kemmis, J. and Tuntstill, J. (1987) *In Care in North Battersea*, Guildford, University of Surrey

Black and in Care (1984) *Black and in Care: Conference Report*, Blackrose Press

Boss, P. and Homeshaw, J. (1975) 'Britain's Black Citizens: A Comparative Study of Social Work with Coloured Families and their White Indigenous Neighbours', *Social Work Today*, vol.6, no. 12

**Bibliography**

Boss, P. and Homeshaw, J. (1974) *Coloured Families and Social Services Departments*, Research Report, University of Leicester, School of Social Work.

Bryman, A. (1988) *Quantity and Quality in Social Research*, Unwin Hyman Ltd.

Burke, A. (1986) 'Racism, Prejudice and Mental Illness', in Cox, J. (ed), *Transcultural Psychiatry*, Croom Helm

Butt, J; Gorbach, P. and Ahmad, B. (1994) *Equally Fair*, Race Equality Unit/National Institute of Social Work (REU/NISW)

Caesar, G., Parchment, M., Berridge, D. and Gordon, G. (994) *Black Perspectives on Services for Children and Young People in Need and their Families*, National Children's Bureau

Carby, H. (1982) 'Schooling in Babylon', in CCCS, *The Empire Strikes Back, Race and Racism in 70s Britain*, Hutchinson

Cawson, P. (1977) *Black Children in Approved Schools*, Department of Health and Social Security

Central Council For Education and Training in Social Work (1991) *Setting the Context for Change*, Anti-Racist Social Work Education, CCETSW

Cheetham, J. (1972) *Social Work with Immigrants*, Routledge and Kegan Paul

Cheetham, J. (1981) *Social Work Services for Ethnic Minorities in Britain and the USA*, Department of Health and Social Security

Cheetham, J. (1982) 'Positive Discrimination in Social Work: Negotiating the Opposition', *New Community*, vol 10, no.1

Cheetham, J. (1982) *Social Work and Ethnicity*, Allen and Unwin

Cheetham, J. (1981) *Social and Community Work in a Multi-Racial Society*, Harper & Row

Cheetham, J. (1989) 'Values in Action', in S. Shardlow, (ed) *The Values of Change in Social Work*, Tavistock/ Routledge

Cleaver, H. and Freeman, P. (1993) *Parental Perspectives in Suspected Child Abuse*, Report submitted to the Department of Health

Cliffe, D. with Berridge, D. (1991) *Closing Children's Homes, An end to Residential Childcare*, NCB

Coleman, D. and Salt, J. (eds) (1996) *Ethnicity in the 1991 Census*, HMSO

Commission for Racial Equality (1977) *A Home from Home? Some Policy Considerations on Black Children in Residential Care*, London: CRE

Commission for Racial Equality/Association of Directors of Social Services (1978) *Multiracial Britain: The Social Services Response*, London:CRE/ADSS

Commission for Racial Equality, EEC Labour Force Survey (1981) *Ethnic Minorities in Britain: Statistical Information on the Pattern of Settlement*, CRE

Commission for Racial Equality (1985) *Immigration Control Procedures: Report of a Formal Investigation*, CRE

Commission for Racial Equality (1989) *Race Equality in Social Services Departments, A Survey of Opportunity Policies*, CRE

Commission for Racial Equality (1995) *Racial Equality Means Quality*, CRE

Connelly, N (1990) *Between Apathy and Outrage: Voluntary Organisations in Multiracial Britain*, Policy Studies Institute

Dale, D. (1987) *Denying Homes to Black Children: Britain's New Race Policies*, Social Affairs Unit, Research Report 8

Dean, C. (1993) *The Arguments for and Against Transracial Placements*, Social Work Monographs

Department of Health and Social Security (1985) *Social Work Decisions in Child Care: Recent Research Findings and their Implications*, HMSO.

Department of Health (1989) *The Care of Children: Principles and Practice in Regulations and Guidance*, HMSO

Department of Health (1991) *The Children Act 1989 Guidance and Regulations*, HMSO

Department of Health (1991) *The Children Act 1989 Guidance and Regulations*, *Volume 1 – Court Orders*, HMSO

Department of Health (1991) *The Children Act 1989 Guidance and Regulations*, *Volume 2 – Family Support, Day Care and Educational Provision for Young Children*, HMSO

Department of Health (1991) *The Children Act 1989 Guidance and Regulations*, *Volume 3 – Family Placement*, HMSO

Department of Health (1991) *The Children Act 1989 Guidance and Regulations*, *Volume 4 – Residential Care*, HMSO

Department of Health (1991) *The Children Act 1989 Guidance and Regulations*, *Volume 5 – Independent Schools*, HMSO

Department of Health (1991) *The Children Act 1989 Guidance and Regulations*, *Volume 6 – Children with Disabilities*, HMSO

Department of Health (1991) *The Children Act 1989 Guidance and Regulations*, *Volume 7 – Guardians Ad Litem and Other Court Related Issues*, HMSO

Department of Health (1991) *The Children Act 1989 Guidance and Regulations*, *Volume 8 – Private Fostering and Miscellaneous*, HMSO

Department of Health (1991) *The Children Act 1989 Guidance and Regulations*, *Volume 9 – Adoption Issues*, HMSO

Department of Health (1993) *Adoption: The Future*

Divine, D. (1983) 'Defective, Hypocritical and Patronising Research', *in Caribbean Times*, 4th March.

Divine, D. (1983) 'No Problems', Article on Gill and Jackson's Research Study, *Caribbean Times*, Feb/March.

Divine, D. (1985) *Submission to the Jasmine Beckford Inquiry Report*, June

Dominelli, L. (1988) *Anti-Racist Social Work*, Macmillan/British Association of Social Workers

Dutt, R. (1994) 'Black Children and Child Protection – Some General Issues', in A. Jones, (ed) *The Role of Black Women in Child Protection*, REU/NISW

Family Rights Group (1991) *The Children Act 1989:Working in Partnership with Families – Trainers Pack*, FRG/HMSO

Fernando, S. (1991) *Mental Health, Race and Culture*, Macmillan

Fernando, S. (1988) *Race and Culture in Psychiatry*, Croom Helm

Fewster, C. (1990) 'The Great Wall of Silence', *Social Work Today*, 21(23), 15 Feb

First Key (1987) *A Study of Black Young People Leaving Care*, CRE

Fitzherbert, K. (1967) *West Indian Children In London*, Bell and Sons

Fitzgerald, J. (1981) 'Black Parents for Black Children', in *Adoption and Fostering*, 5, 110–11, BAAF

Foren, R. and Batta, I. (1970) ' "Colour" as a Variable in the Use made of a Local Authority Child Care Department', *Social Work*, 27(3), 10–15

Gibbons, J; Conroy, S. and Bell, C. (1995) *Operating the Child Protection System*, HMSO

Gilroy, P. (1987) *There ain't no Black in the Union Jack*, Hutchinson

Gilroy, P. (1993) *Small Acts*, Serpent's Tail

Gill, O. and Jackson, B. (1983) *Adoption and Race*, Batsford/BAAF

Hayes, M. (1987) 'Placing Black Children', in *Adoption and Fostering*, 11(3), 14–16, BAAF

Hardiker, P; Exton, K.. and Barker, M. (1991) *Policies and Practices in Preventive Child Care*, Avebury

Ho, M. K. (1987) *Family Therapy with Ethnic Minorities*, Sage publications

Horn, E. (1982) 'A Survey of Referrals from Asian families to Four Social Services Area Offices in Bradford', in J.Cheetham (ed) *Social Work and Ethnicity*, Allen and Unwin

Humphries, B. and Truman, C. (1994) *Rethinking Social Research*, Avebury

Hussain, N (forthcoming) 'Working with South Asian Young Women', in R. Barn (ed) *Direct Work with Black Children and Young People*, BAAF

Jackson, B. (1976) *Family Experiences of Interracial Adoption*, Association of British Adoption Agencies

James, M. (1981) 'Finding the Families', in *Adoption and Fostering*, 5, 1:11–16, BAAF

Jansari, A. (1980) 'Social Work with Ethnic Minorities: A Review of the Literature', *Multiracial Social Work*, 1, 17–34

Johnson, M.R.D. (1986) 'Citizenship, Social Work and Ethnic Minorities', in Etherington, S. (ed) *Social Work and Citizenship*, British Association of Social Workers

Jones, A. and Butt, J. (1995) *Taking the Initiative: The Report of a National Study Assessing Service Provision to Black Families and Children*, NSPCC

Jones, C. (1983) *State Social Work and the Working Class*, Macmillan

Kaniuk, J. (1991) 'Strategies in Recruiting Black Adopters', in *Adoption and Fostering*, 15, 1:38–39, BAAF

Kay, J. (1991) *The Adoption Papers*, Blood Axe Books

Knapp, M (1984) *The Economics of Social Care*, Macmillan

Kornreich, R. et al (1973) *Social Workers' Attitudes Towards Immigrant Clients, A Summary of the Research Project*, School of Applied Social Studies, University of Bradford

Lambeth Directorate of Social Services (1981) *Black Children in Care*, N. Adams, Research Section

Lambert, J. (1970) *Crime, Police and Race Relations*, Oxford University Press

Lane, J. (1993) 'What role has the law played in getting rid of racism in the lives of children?' *in Children & Society*, 7(2), 164–182

Lawrence, E. (1981) 'Common Sense, Racism and the Sociology of Race Relations', Centre for Contemporary Cultural Studies, Stencilled Occasional Paper, no. 66.

Lindley, B. (1994) *On the Receiving End: Families' Experiences of the Court Process in Care and Supervision Proceedings under the Children Act 1989*, Final Report, FRG

Macdonald, S. (1991) *All Equal Under the Act*, REU/NISW

McCulloch, J. and Smith, N. (1974) 'Black and Social Work', *New Society*, 25 April

McCulloch, J, Smith, N. and Batta, I. (1979) 'Colour as a Variable in the Children's Section of a Local Authority Social Services Department', *New Community*, 7, 78–84

Malahleka, S. and Wolfe, B. (1991) Ethnically Sensitive Social Work: The Obstacle Race', *in Practice*, 5:1, 47–64

Maximé, J. (1993) 'The Importance of Racial Identity for Psychological Well Being of Black Children', in *Association of Child Psychology and Psychiatry Newsletter*, 15 (4), 173–179

Milner, D. (1983) Children and Race, *Ten Years On*, Allen Sutton

National Association for the Care and Resettlement of Offenders (1989) *Black People and the Criminal Justice System, A Report of the NACRO Race Issues National Advisory Committee*, NACRO

National Children's Home (1954) 'The Problem of the Coloured Child: The Experience of the National Children's Home', *Child Care Quarterly*, 8 (2)

Office for National Statistics (1996) *Social Focus on Ethnic Minorities*, HMSO

Ohri, S. (1988) 'Politics of Racism, Statistics and Equal Opportunity', in A. Bhatt, R. Carr-Hill and S. Ohri, Britain's Black Population: *A New Perspective*, 2nd edition, Gower

Ousley, M. et al (1981) *The System*, Runnymede Trust and South London Equal Rights Consultancy Publications

Owen, D. (1992) *Ethnic Minorities in Great Britain*, 1991 Census Statistical paper No. 1

Packman, J., Randall, J. and Jacques, N. (1986) *Who Needs Care – Social Work Decision about Childern*, Basil Blackwell

Paniagua, F. A. (1994) *Assessing and Treating Culturally Diverse Clients*, Sage Publications

## Bibliography

Pearce, K.S. (1974) 'West Indian Boys in Community Home Schools', Unpublished Thesis for the Diploma in the Educational Rehabilitation of Young People, University of London, Institute of Education, Published in Abridged Form in *Community Schools Gazette*, 68(6)(7)(8)

Pinder, R. and Shaw, M. (1974) *Coloured Children in Long Term Care*, Unpublished Report, University of Leicester, School of Social Work

Pinder, R. (1982) *Encountering Diversity: Observations on the Social Work Assessment of Black Children*, University of Leeds, Centre for Social Work and Applied Social Studies, Occasional Paper. No 9

Rapoport, R. (1985) (ed) *Children, Youth and Families – The Action Research Relationship*, Cambridge University Press

Raynor, L. (1970) *Adoption of Non-White Children: The Experiences of a British Adoption Project*, Allen and Unwin

Richards, B. (1989) Family, Race and Identity, in *Adoption and Fostering*, 11:3, 10–13, BAAF

Rowe, J. and Lambert, L. (1973) *Children Who Wait*, Association of British Adoption Agencies

Rowe, J., Hundleby, M. and Garnett, L. (1989) *Child Care Now*, BAAF

Rowe, J. (1990) 'Research, Race and Child Care Placements', in *Adoption and Fostering*, 14:2, 6–8, BAAF

Rhodes, P. (1992) *Racial Matching in Fostering*, Avebury

Sinclair, R; Garnett, L. and Berridge, D. (1995) *Social Work and Assessment with Adolescents*, NCB

Small, J. (1982) 'New Black Families', *Adoption and Fostering*, 6, 3:35, BAAF

Small, J. (1984) 'The Crisis in Adoption', *International Journal of Psychiatry*, 30, Spring, 129-142

Smith, P. and Berridge, D. (1994) *Ethnicity and Child Care Placements*, NCB

Social Services Inspectorate, Department of Health (1990) *Child Care Policy: Putting it in Writing*, HMSO

Stubbs, P. (1991) 'The Children Act: An Anti-Racist Perspective', in *Practice*, 5:3, 226–229

Thoburn, J; Lewis, A. and Shemmings, D. (1995) *Paternalism or Partnership? Family Involvement in the Child Protection Process*, HMSO

Tipler, J. (1986) *Is Justice Colour Blind? A Study of the Impact of Race in the Juvenile Justice System in Hackney*, Social Services Research Note 6

Tizard, B. and Phoenix, P. (1993) *Black, White or Mixed-Race*, Routledge

Tower Hamlets Directorate of Social Services (1982) *Children Who Come into Care in Tower Hamlets*, A. Wilkinson, London Borough of Tower Hamlets

Triseliotis, J. (1983) 'Identity and Security in Adoption and Long-term Fostering' in *Adoption and Fostering*, 7:1, 22–31, BAAF

Walker, M. A. (1988) 'The Court Disposal of Young Males, by Race, in London in 1983', *British Journal of Criminology*

**Bibliography**

# Index

# Q

qualitative case studies, 18–19
quantitative file study, 17–18
questionnaires, 18

# R

Race Relations Act (1976), 12–14, 26, 77, 94
racism awareness training, 28, 82, 92, 95
Raynor, L, 7, 9
referral process
    sources of referral, 37–38
    reasons for referral, 38–40
religion, 36
research authorities
    pen pictures, 21–22
    ethnic composition, 22–24
    social services departments, 24–26
    policies, 26–31
research methodology, 2, 16–20
research sample children
    characteristics, 35–38
    ethnic background, 33
residential care, 7–9, 11, 68–69, 75, 91, 96
Robson, C, 16
Rowe, J, 1, 4, 5, 7,  23, 53, 63, 67

# S

schools, 38, 40
sexual abuse, 39, 40, 42, 48, 49, 57, 73
Sikh, 36
Sinclair, R, 81
Small, J, 10
Smith, P, 10

social services departments
    allocation policies, 30–31, 41
    equal opportunities policies, 26–28
    placement policies, 29
    research teams, 24–26
Social Services Inspectorate, 29, 68
social workers
    ethnic background, 40–41
    interviews with, 19
    sex, 41
socio-economic circumstances, 37, 43
Stubbs, P, 11

# T

terminology and definitions 2
Thoburn, J, 85
Tipler, J, 6
Tizard, B, 10, 71
Tower Hamlet Directorate of Social Services, 4
transracial placements, 10, 68, 69

# V

Vietnamese children, 2, 19, 62

# W

Walker, M. A, 6
White
    children, 2, 4, 19, 22, 23, 34, 35
    child protection, 48, 49
    looked after, 55–58
    placement, 67–68
    social workers, 25–26
Wilson, M. B, 77

# British Agencies for Adoption and Fostering

British Agencies for Adoption and Fostering (BAAF) is the leading organisation with a national voice promoting best practice in adoption and fostering services for children separated from their birth families. BAAF is a registered charity whose income is derived from membership subscriptions, training and consultancy charges, publication sales, family finding fees, grants and donations.

## What does BAAF do?

- BAAF promotes and develops high standards in adoption and fostering for child care, medical, legal and other relevant professionals. We produce a range of standard setting publications and offer a highly regarded training programme which includes specialist and multidisciplinary workshops, seminars and conferences held nationally and through five BAAF regional centres in Scotland, Wales and England.

- BAAF promotes public and professional understanding of adoption and of the life-long implications for children separated from their birth families, including the racial, cultural, religious and linguistic needs of children and young people separated from their birth families.

- BAAF acts as an independent voice in the field of child care, to inform and influence policy makers and legislators, and all those responsible for the welfare of children and young people.

- BAAF provides a child placement consultancy including finding families for children through our successful computerised BAAF*Link* service and our widely circulated *Be My Parent* publications.

- BAAF works within a child centred, multidisciplinary and anti-discriminatory framework, working with all statutory agencies and voluntary organisations concerned with child care, but with a focus on fostering and adoption. Our Black Issues Project ensures a continued emphasis is placed on the placement needs of black children, including children of mixed parentage.

## BAAF members

BAAF's corporate membership includes nearly every local authority in Scotland, Wales and England and all voluntary adoption agencies. Associate corporate members include independent fostering agencies, overseas agencies, including those in Northern Ireland, and other organisations working in the child care field. If you would like more information on corporate membership please contact the Membership Officer at our Head Office.

BAAF's individual membership is composed of people from many areas and is a reflection of the multidisciplinary nature of adoption, fostering and child care work. They include social workers, practitioners in the medical and legal professions, psychologists, psychiatrists, counsellors, carers and adopters, guardians *ad litem*, students and academics.

**Head Office**
Skyline House
200 Union Street
London SE1 0LX
Tel: 0171 593 2000
Fax: 0171 593 2001

*Also at Head Office:*
**Be My Parent**
**Publications Department**
**Black Issues Project**
**Membership Department**

**Scottish Centre**
40 Shandwick Place
Edinburgh EH2 4RT
Tel: 0131 225 9285
Fax: 0131 226 3778

**Welsh Centre**
7 Cleeve House
Lambourne Crescent
Cardiff CF4 5GJ
Tel: 01222 761155

**Central and Northern Region**
St. George's House
Coventry Road
Coleshill
Birmingham B46 3EA
Tel: 01675 463998/464168
Fax: 01675 465620

*and at:*
Grove Villa
82 Cardigan Road
Headingley
Leeds LS6 3BJ
Tel: 0113 274 4797
Fax: 0113 278 0492

*and at:*
MEA House
Ellison Place
Newcastle-upon-Tyne NE1 8XS
Tel: 0191 261 6600
Fax: 0191 232 2063

**Southern Region**
Skyline House
200 Union Street
London SE1 0LX
Tel: 0171 593 2041
Fax: 0171 593 2001 (Head Office fax)

**BAAF*Link***
MEA House
Ellison Place
NEWCASTLE-UPON-TYNE
NE1 8XS
Tel: 0191 232 3200
Fax: 0191 232 2063

# The Commission for Racial Equality

The Commission for Racial Equality (CRE) was set up under the 1976 Race Relations Act. It receives an annual grant from the Home Office, but works independently of Government. The CRE is run by Commissioners appointed by the Home Secretary, and has support from all the main political parties.

The CRE has three main duties:

- To work towards the elimination of racial discrimination and to promote equality of opportunity.

- To encourage good relations between people from different racial backgrounds.

- To monitor the way the Race Relations Act is working and recommend ways in which it can be improved.

The CRE is working for a just society which gives everyone an equal chance to learn, work and live free from discrimination and prejudice, and from the fear of racial harassment and violence.


## What the CRE does
The CRE works in both the public and private sectors: in employment, training, trade unions, housing, goods and services, social security, education, social services, health, policing, legal services and the criminal justice system.

### Enforcing the law
Using its powers under the Race Relations Act, the CRE

- Directly advises and assists people with complaints of racial discrimination or puts them in touch with other agencies that will help.

- Conducts formal investigations of companies and organisations where there is evidence of possible discrimination. If the investigation does find discrimination, the CRE can make the organisation change the way it operates.

- Takes legal action in cases involving racially discriminatory job advertisements. The CRE also takes action against organisations (such as employment agencies) that attempt to pressurise or persuade others to discriminate.

### Promoting equal opportunities and good race relations
The CRE also:

- Issues codes of practice and racial equality standards to help organisations develop fair policies, procedures and practices.

- Advises employers, local authorities, housing, health and education authorities, the police, training bodies and other agencies on how to avoid discrimination.

- Helps to fund a network of Racial Equality Councils (RECs). The RECs are managed by representatives of community groups, voluntary and statutory organisations, and individuals who support their aims.

- Advises, and makes representations to government on race issues. It keeps MPs, MEPs, political parties, national bodies and the media informed.

- Initiates public education campaigns to raise awareness of race issues, and encourages others to play their part in creating a just society.

## CRE publications

For a complete catalogue of CRE booklets, guides, reports, posters, and leaflets, or for any of our free publications please send a stamped and self-addressed A4 envelope to:

CRE Distribution Services
Elliot House
10–12 Allington Street
London
SW1E 5EH

The catalogue contains full details of how to order priced publications.

## CRE offices

**London** *(Head Office)*
Elliot House, 10–12 Allington Street, London SW1E 5EH

**Birmingham**
Alpha Tower (11th floor), Suffolk Street Queensway, Birmingham B1 1TT

**Leeds**
Yorkshire Bank Chambers (1st floor), Infirmary Street, Leeds LS1 2JP

**Manchester**
Maybrook House (5th floor), 40 Blackfriars Street, Manchester M3 2EG

**Leicester**
Haymarket House (4th floor), Haymarket Shopping Centre, Leicester LE1 3YG

**Scotland**
Hanover House, 45 Hanover Street, Edinburgh EH2 2PJ

**Wales**
Pearl Assurance House (14th floor), Greyfriars Street, Cardiff CF1 3AG